GOOD GIRL, BAD GIRL

GOOD GIRL, BAD GIRL

An Insider's Biography of Whitney Houston

Kevin Ammons

WITH

Nancy Bacon

A BIRCH LANE PRESS BOOK
Published by Carol Publishing Group

A Birch Lane Press Book
Published by Carol Publishing Group
Birch Lane Press is a registered trademark of Carol Communications, Inc.
Editorial, sales and distribution, rights and permissions inquiries should be addressed to Carol Publishing Group, 120 Enterprise Avenue, Secaucus, N.J. 07094

In Canada: Canadian Manda Group, One Atlantic Avenue, Suite 105, Toronto, Ontario M6K 3E7

Carol Publishing Group books may be purchased in bulk at special discounts for sales promotion, fund-raising, or educational purposes. Special editions can be created to specifications. For details, contact Special Sales Department, 120 Enterprise Avenue, Secaucus, N.J. 07094.

Manufactured in the United States of America
10 9 8 7 6 5 4 3 2 1

Library of Congress Cataloging-in-Publication Data

Ammons, Kevin.
    Good girl, bad girl : an insider's biography of Whitney Houston / Kevin Ammons with Nancy Bacon.
        p.   cm.
    Includes index.
    ISBN 1-55972-379-3 (hardcover)
    1. Houston, Whitney.   2. Singers—United States—Biography.
I.   Bacon, Nancy, 1940–   . II. Title.
ML420.H675A66   1996
782.42164'092—dc20
    [B]   96-27167
                                                                CIP
                                                                MN

This book is dedicated
with love to
Sherlena Ammons
&
Staci Layne Wilson

With a very special thanks to Carol Chant and Peter Viser.

Contents

GOOD GIRL, BAD GIRL

1

How I Met
Whitney Houston

OCTOBER 27, 1991, WAS THE MOST EXHILARATING, EXCITING NIGHT of my life. I was in Los Angeles to attend the Thirteenth Annual Black Achievement Awards, sitting front row center, a guest of Whitney Houston's. The huge room was packed with celebrities. Klieg lights arced off the women's jewels. Most every African American who had ever starred in a movie or sang a hit song was there, all decked out in finery, faces alight with anticipation. And there I was, a kid from the projects in Chicago who had grown up admiring the very people I now sat next to.

I stood and cheered when Patti LaBelle strode center stage and announced she would be singing her new release, "Somebody Loves You, Baby." As the band struck the first note, the cheering almost drowned them out, but soon Patti's smoky voice rose above the roar, and the crowd quieted to listen. I was not ten feet away from one of the most beautiful women I'd ever seen, and I felt my heart lurch as her eyes sought and held my gaze. She was wearing a tight black velvet top, cut to a deep V to expose a creamy expanse of cleavage, and her black net skirt was puffy, stopping just above her dimpled knees. As she swayed and danced her way down the length of the T-shaped stage, her gaze caught mine again. Then she stopped directly in front of me and waggled her fingers at me. "Come on, baby," she said. "Do it—stand up, baby, and do it—like this." She was swaying just inches from my face, the bell-shaped skirt hypnotizing me, her beckoning fingers urging me from my seat. I stood and began swaying with her in time with the music. The crowd roared its approval and Patti said, "Come on, baby, dance with me."

To this day I don't remember actually climbing up on that stage, but I must have because the next thing I knew, I was dancing with Patti LaBelle, feeling her hands flirt across my fingers and arms as she said again, "Dance, baby, come on. Sing with me—move, baby, like this." And I was moving. I was dancing. I was singing with Patti LaBelle. The roar of the crowd completely intoxicated me and loosened my inhibitions, and my voice soared above it as I joined Patti in the words of the song. But instead of singing "Oh, baby, oh, baby" as she was, I sang, "Oh, Patti, oh, Patti," and the crowd stomped and cheered even louder. Patti's arms slipped around my waist, and she pulled me close, singing, dancing, moving against me as our voices intertwined in harmony. She turned to grin at the audience. "He's bad," she said, then faced me and teased, "Ohhh, baby, I'm scared of you!"

As the song came to an end, I started moving offstage, but Patti grabbed my hand and asked, "What's your name, honey?" I managed to croak, "Kevin Ammons."

"Kevin," she repeated, raising her arm to the crowd in a gesture of introduction.

My head was still reeling when I went backstage after the show to meet up with Whitney. I had been dating Whitney's publicist, Regina Brown, for several months and had met Whitney a few times before. She was looking at me with a new expression of respect and interest. I had always aspired to a singing career and had shared this dream with Regina, but apparently she had not mentioned it to Whitney.

Patti came up to me and commented again on what a good singer I was. She asked me if I was signed with anyone and did I have representation. "If not," she said, "I'd be interested in discussing management with you."

Before I had a chance to answer, Whitney came rushing over and said, "Yes, he does. *I'm* going to manage him."

This was big news to me, and I was understandably flabbergasted. I stood there, looking back and forth between the two divas, and I actually felt the competitive heat between them. This was my first experience with the control freak who lived just beneath the cool surface of Whitney Houston. As I got to know her better, I saw firsthand how she wielded her power and insisted on getting her way. If someone else wanted something, Whitney wanted it more and would move mountains to get it. Once the chase was over, she was no longer interested.

But on that headiest of all nights, I didn't know this and I was impressed and ecstatic. I felt I was finally going to make it. The dream I had dreamed all of my life was there in front of me, in the breathtakingly beautiful superstar Whitney Houston. She was going to manage my singing career and make me a star. She promised me quality demos, a band, backup singers, studio time, the whole nine yards, and I believed every word she said. I was walking on air by the time Regina and I got back to our hotel suite, and all the while we were making love, I was hearing in my head the sound of the audience applauding.

But it didn't happen. Whitney put me off time and again, making such lame excuses that I soon became embarrassed even to be in the same room with her. I was hurt and confused and would often ask Regina what the hell was going on, but there were no answers there, either. As my affair with Regina intensified, it became clear to me that Whitney didn't want to see me succeed as a performer. She wanted to keep me right where I was—at her beck and call. In retrospect, I'm ashamed to admit that I allowed myself to be sucked into the Whitney Machine (or the Royal Family as she liked to refer to everyone who worked for her), but I rationalized it to myself because I wanted stardom so badly.

I couldn't remember a time when I *didn't* want to sing. My father sang with the Blenders, and my mother was one of the Five Dolls in her own all-female group. As kids growing up in the hardscrabble projects of Chicago, my siblings and I would fall asleep every night listening to my parents rehearse. From birth, we knew the Ammons name had a musical legacy attached to it. There was my uncle Albert Ammons, the pianist and boogie-woogie king, and my cousin Gene "Jug" Ammons, tenor saxophone player. Who knows how far my father might have gone if he hadn't succumbed to alcoholism. By the time I was fifteen years old in 1974, he had drunk himself to death. His death was listed as a coronary thrombosis, but everyone knew that booze had rotted his soul.

I was born February 5, 1959, in Chicago. My parents were living with my father's sister in the projects that housed mostly junkies. My aunt was a heroin addict, and one of my earliest memories (only because it was told so often during my growing-up years, I came to believe that I actually remembered the event myself) was when I was just a toddler still in diapers. An undercover cop had purchased a bag of heroin from my aunt and had followed her home. She had just entered the apartment and was on the nod from shooting up when a loud banging shook my tiny world. "Police!" a voice shouted as the pounding on the door intensified. "Open this fucking door! Police!"

The next thing I knew I was being scooped up in my father's strong arms. He shoved something down inside my diaper. I later learned he had quickly grabbed his sister's stash of drugs and hidden them in the only place he could think of. My mother opened the door and the cramped room was suddenly filled with police officers—guns drawn, demanding to know where the dope was hidden. My parents protested their innocence and invited the officers to search, which they did—and found nothing. My mother tells me that I was such a happy-go-lucky, good-hearted little baby I laughed and gurgled, holding out my chubby arms to the officers, and the cops couldn't resist pausing in their search to tickle me and compliment her on what a pretty baby she had.

Eight months later my aunt was dead of a drug-related cardiac arrest, and my parents moved the family to another run-down tenement where life wasn't much better, financially. But it *was* better emotionally. Our new neighborhood was just as dangerous as the old one had been, with gang violence, prostitution, and drug dealing being the careers of choice, so my siblings and I didn't play outside very often. My mother devised inside games to amuse us, and we often put on musical shows or joined in when my parents were rehearsing with their bands. The main thing I remember about my childhood was that it was filled with music.

Many years later, when I met Whitney Houston and we began swapping childhood stories, I was amazed at the similarity of our backgrounds. We were both poor black kids, growing up in the ghettos, struggling every day just to stay alive. Both of our families were dysfunctional, but I think I fared better, emotionally, than Whitney did. My mother is a loving, gentle but strong-willed woman who kept a sharp eye on all her children, and pity the poor fool who tried to do us any harm.

Whitney and her brother, Michael, were latchkey kids, left alone daily to fend for themselves while both their parents worked. Whitney admits she was lonely and afraid much of the time, and angry, too, that her mother didn't seem to care enough about her to be there for her. Other children were just as poor as she was, but they had mothers waiting for them after school. Whitney didn't and to this day it's a resentment that festers.

That her mother, Cissy Houston, was a celebrity in the neighborhood didn't matter all that much to a little girl. She wanted her mother home, not in some club entertaining other people. Cissy had always been a gospel singer in her church and had enjoyed small successes over the years as a popular rhythm-and-blues artist, but it wasn't until after Whitney was born that her career really took off. She formed her own group, the Sweet Inspirations. Soon they were appearing regularly at the Apollo, Philharmonic Hall, and any of a dozen nightclubs and theaters. Which meant that Cissy's days were taken up with rehearsal and her nights were spent performing, so there wasn't much time left over for her children. In Cissy's defense, it should be noted that she worked long and hard for a career she prayed would move her family up in the world. To get them out of the projects and into a house of their own was a dream she clung to, and if it meant not being with her kids as much as she would have liked, so be it. Cissy was (and still is) a religious woman, and she admits to leaving her children in God's protective care while she pursued her dream. But to little kids such as Michael and Whitney, that must have been pretty confusing. God wasn't sitting in an easy chair waiting for them when they came home from school. He didn't cook their dinner or ask them how their day had been. He couldn't read them a bedtime story or tuck them in and kiss them good night. Only a mother could do those things.

Whitney says that it took her a long time to come to terms with her lonely childhood. As she grew older, she realized that both her parents had to work to keep a roof over their heads and food on the table. She understood her mother's desperate desire to become a star because it would have helped the family move out of the projects and into a better, safer neighborhood.

2

A Miracle on Seventh Avenue

IN SUMMER IN THE EAST, WHITE-HOT SUN BLISTERS THE SIDEWALKS and the intense humidity causes sweat to pour off your body seconds after you step out of the shower. Not even a trace of a breeze ruffles the sweltering smog. Local weathermen, trying for levity, announce, "It's *so* humid today, you're gonna have to wring out the air before you breathe it!"

On just such an oppressively hot day on August 9, 1963, Cissy Houston went into labor. Her husband, John, took her to the hospital, then waited in the "fathers' room" while Cissy made herself comfortable in the coolness of her own room. She was watching television (and timing her contractions) when the popular sitcom *Hazel* flashed across the screen. The series star was the irrepressible Shirley Booth, but the second female lead, Whitney Blake, caught and held Cissy's attention. She was cool, elegant, classy, and smart. Then and there, Cissy decided that if her baby was a girl, she'd name her Whitney—and pray that she would grow up to be as successful as her namesake. A few hours later Whitney Elizabeth Houston made her debut. The power of her lusty little lungs seemed to foretell her destiny.

Cissy had always thought that her own destiny was pre-ordained and that she would somehow waltz right into super-stardom as a gospel singer. She had grown up surrounded by music and could not remember a time when she didn't sing. One of five children, her birth name was Emily Drinkard, but family and friends had always called her Cissy. Her parents encouraged all the children to sing, so they created their own group, the Drinkard Singers, and performed in different churches every weekend. They also did a little backup singing and recorded a few songs for both RCA and Savoy Records. But they were not making enough money to give up their day jobs, and the whole family had to work to support themselves.

Cissy was married, briefly and disastrously, and gave birth to a son, Gary. Nothing is known about this early union, and to this day Cissy refuses to comment. But it must have been pretty bad because she swore off men and marriage and dedicated herself completely to her music. She was a young woman in the late fifties, a time of exciting change and revolution. The civil rights movement was just around the corner, but what excited Cissy more was that the airwaves were filled with records made by black artists—many of them black *female* artists!

She felt her time had finally come, and she threw herself headlong into her career. She formed another group, the Drinkard Sisters, with her sister Marie, her cousin Lee Warrick Drinkard, and Lee's two daughters, Marie Dionne and Dee Dee Warrick. The breakout star of this modest little singing group was Marie Dionne, who dropped her first name, changed the spelling of her last name, and tried to make it as a solo artist as Dionne Warwick. She would succeed beyond her wildest expectations.

Cissy Houston went on to sing backup for many other groups, but she never became the big star that she felt she should be. Enter John Houston, a charismatic, handsome, sometime singer from Trenton, New Jersey, who filled Cissy's head with promises of fame and fortune. He sincerely believed she would become a huge star and convinced her not only to let him manage her career, but also to marry him. He must have been one hell of a charmer, given Cissy's leeriness of men and marriage, but he won her over and they were wed.

Cissy's son Gary lived with them, of course, and they soon had another son, Michael, followed a couple of years later by little Whitney Elizabeth. Cissy continued to tour and sing wherever she could through both of her pregnancies, and when the babies were born, she left them with John or family members and doggedly pursued her dream of stardom.

Her niece, Dionne Warwick, had been discovered by Burt Bacharach and had secured a contract with Scepter Records. The next few years saw her hit the charts with such memorable tunes as "Don't Make Me Over," "Alfie," "I Say a Little Prayer for You," "Message to Michael," and "Do You Know the Way to San Jose?"

Cissy always believed *she* had a much better voice than any of the women she sang with during those early years and seethed inside that no one else recognized it.

Dionne's success made Cissy more determined than ever to become a superstar in her own right. And with her husband encouraging her, pushing her, lining up gigs as well as recording sessions, she just knew it was only a matter of time before she became the singing sensation she already knew she was.

It didn't happen.

The sixties were a time of racial strife over much of the United States, and Newark became a battleground of hatred and violence. In 1967, a riot resulted in dozens of deaths, hundreds of injuries, and climaxed in fires that reduced much of Newark to rubble. The Houston family clung together in their small apartment, watching the frightening destruction on television. When the flames died down, it was estimated that property damage amounted to well over $10 million.

John Houston acted swiftly. Some buildings were still smoldering when he packed up his family and moved them as far away as he could afford, to suburban East Orange. This was a middle-class, mixed-race neighborhood, paradise compared to the mean streets of the projects where Whitney had been born. It was also more expensive, and Cissy hit the road again, this time with a group, formed in 1965, called Cissy's Girls. They were still backup singers (recording background vocals), for such big artists as Dusty Springfield, Leslie Uggams, Connie Francis, Buddy Rich, Wilson Pickett, and Cissy's own niece, Dionne Warwick.

Cissy's Girls were good and therefore in constant demand, but they were paid little for their musical contributions, which ate away at their egos—especially Cissy's. She still believed that her voice was superior to that of every other female singer out there, and she chafed to be recognized. *She* wanted to be the one standing out front, clutching that microphone, strutting her stuff on-stage to cheers and whistles of admiration. A session singer's job is to make the star look good, and this didn't sit well with Cissy. "It was frustrating to watch someone else take all the glory for our work," she said.

John agreed. It was time to make a major move. Between 1965 and 1967, Cissy's Girls sang backup for a few of Aretha Franklin's records, and producer Jerry Wexler was impressed. "They were truly inspirational," he said, "their voices as pure as angels." So in June 1967 he renamed Cissy's Girls the Sweet Inspirations and signed them to a contract with Atlantic Records. Their first album, aptly titled *Sweet Inspiration*, produced a Top-Twenty single, and Cissy thought this time for sure she was on her way straight to the top.

For the next two years the Sweet Inspirations toured with Aretha Franklin and finally realized success in their own right. In 1968 they sang backup for Elvis Presley and their star shone even brighter. It was a heady time for Cissy and John as they felt their dream was about to come true. Cissy was almost always in a recording session, and she began taking Whitney with her.

Aretha Franklin remembers meeting her when Whitney was about five years old. "She was always there, in my face," she told Jeffrey Bowman, author of *Diva*. "I loved her. She wanted to sing. I knew that even then. She was always watching closely,

12

whispering to her mother. She had great spirit. She sang in the corner, always humming to herself, trying to duplicate the sounds she was hearing. She'd say, 'I want to be a Sweet Inspiration, too.' "

Cissy was a strict mother and insisted on total obedience from her children, but when she brought Whitney to recording sessions, the little girl just couldn't sit still. She would hum or sing along with the recording artists, swaying to the music, trying to match them note for note, until her mother would physically remove her from the studio.

Whitney was beautiful, much more so than any other little girl in her neighborhood. She wasn't as dark as her relatives or friends. Her skin was smooth and creamy, almost as if a teaspoon of chocolate syrup had been dropped into a glass of milk. Her eyes were large and luminous, slightly almond-shaped, giving her an exotic, mysterious look. She never went through the gawky, awkward stage that plagues most teenagers—she simply metamorphosed from adolescence into a stunning teenager.

Whitney was twelve years old when her mother finally gave in to her pleas to sing onstage and arranged for Whitney to solo at the New Hope Baptist Church. Cissy was out of town (as usual) so she wasn't there for her daughter's debut, but John was. He had always called his little girl Nippy, a special love name just between the two of them, although soon other family members and close friends used the name as well. He reported later that the crowd went wild for his Nippy, clapping, whistling, stomping, just about scaring the life out of the young girl, who stood quaking onstage. It was several minutes before Whitney realized they meant her no harm—they were just showing their love and appreciation. And Whitney wrapped that raw outpouring of love and acceptance around herself like a warm, embracing blanket.

For the first time in her life she felt as if she belonged. She had been teased and taunted by her classmates because of her exotic beauty, her light skin, and her prissy manners. Her mother had always dressed her like a little princess, so while the other children in the neighborhood played in the streets in torn jeans and dirty T-shirts, Whitney wore starched dresses and shiny Mary Janes with lace-trimmed anklets.

On more than one occasion she ran home crying, her dress torn and the ribbons yanked from her hair by jealous girls. When she tried to hide behind her mother, Cissy would turn her around and tell her to march right back and give those kids the same "whupping" they'd given her.

"If you don't stand up for yourself and show them you're not afraid, they'll never leave you alone," Cissy would tell the sobbing Whitney. "And the next time I catch you runnin' home bawlin', *I'll* whup you for being a coward!"

So Whitney learned to give as good as she got, and while she never made any friends, at least she earned a grudging respect and could walk home in peace. If she thought elementary school was bad, it was nothing like high school. Because of the racial unrest that still existed in the public school system, John and Cissy decided to send Whitney to a private high school, Mount St. Dominic Academy in Caldwell, New Jersey—an all-girl Catholic school.

Whitney met with hostility and jealousy from the first day. This was the era of black awareness with the byword of the day boldly stating "Black is beautiful," but Whitney wasn't black. In fact, she was lighter than many of the Caucasian girls. With her high cheekbones, straight, narrow nose, exotic almond eyes, and perfectly shaped lips, she stood out like a rose in a tangle of sagebrush.

For all of Cissy's success as a backup singer (and it was impressive all through the sixties and into the seventies) she never became a star in her own right. Personal fame always seemed so near, but it never materialized. She became even more frustrated, angry, and unhappy—and so did John. He blamed himself for not "making it happen" for his wife, and she probably agreed with him. After all, she still believed that her voice was far superior to that of any other female singer on earth. Perhaps this bull-like confidence (or conceit) was her problem, because the popularity of the Sweet Inspirations began a downward slide in the midseventies and they never regained their footing.

14

Even though John still managed Cissy's career and was paid a percentage for his time and talent, they never had enough money to allow him to give up his day jobs completely. When money was tight, he would be back on the streets of Newark working as a day laborer to make ends meet. Where once music and laughter had filled their apartment, now bitter quarreling sent Michael and Whitney scurrying to their rooms.

The marriage ended in 1977 and John moved out, leaving a devastated Nippy feeling abandoned and bewildered. She had always been a daddy's girl and she missed him sorely. To Cissy's credit, she tried to make up for the loss by spending more time with Whitney, taking her with her wherever she went.

In 1978, Whitney turned fifteen, a tall, leggy, gorgeous woman-child with slender curves and the haughty carriage of a young queen. Her natural shyness as well as her early loneliness set her apart, giving her an air of arrogance that was at once both intriguing and off-putting. If someone did try to approach her, she would stop them with a cool, wary look of disdain.

She and her mother were in New York one day, taking in the sights, walking down Seventh Avenue near Carnegie Hall, when (just like in the movies) a talent scout for Click Models approached her with his card. Whitney thought it was all malarkey but Cissy wanted to check it out; this might just be worthwhile. She took Whitney to the agency that afternoon, where she was signed on the spot. Within weeks the teenager was doing layouts for *Mademoiselle, Seventeen,* and other top women's magazines. A few months later she switched to a much larger agency, the internationally known Wilhelmina, and was soon appearing on the pages of *Young Miss, Cosmopolitan, Glamour*—as well as doing print work for Sprite and Revlon cosmetics. *Now* her classmates really had something to be jealous about, and she admits that high school was sheer hell.

With John gone and Cissy's career slipping, Whitney's mother had more time to spend with her children. She was always there for Whitney during the difficult teen years. One summer she suggested that Whitney volunteer to be a counselor at a local camp

15

for children, never dreaming the experience would change her life forever.

Whitney had never had any girlfriends, so when she met Robyn Crawford, another counselor at camp, she was amazed at the instant rapport between them. The girls soon became inseparable. Robyn was two years older than Whitney and fell easily into the role of big sister. In fact, they told everyone they *were* sisters, and wherever you saw one, you saw the other.

It has been reported dozens of times in other publications that Whitney and Robyn's friendship blossomed into love and became the first sexual experience for both of them. (Whitney has emphatically denied any allegations that she is a lesbian.) Kids at camp teased them, calling them "dykes" and making kissing sounds when they passed by, arms linked and heads together in some private, intimate conversation.

But the two girls didn't seem to care. They were both tough, headstrong young women and their relationship was volatile. Robyn was not jealous of Whitney's beauty. She is very pretty, too. Nor was she intimidated by Whitney's singing talent. In fact, she encouraged Whitney to take a chance and see how far her beauty and talent would take her.

And Robyn was right there by her side every step of the way, cheering her on. The friendship that began sixteen years ago is stronger than ever. The special bond between these two women has long fed the gossip mills, but not even the most vicious comments can come between them.

3

The Great Hype

THERE'S NO DOUBT THAT WHITNEY COULD HAVE BECOME ONE OF the top models of all time. She is as beautiful as Beverly Johnson, Iman, or Naomi Campbell, and her love affair with the camera was apparent from the start. But modeling bored Whitney. "Any fool can sit there and grin at the camera," she said. "Where's the talent in that?"

But singing, now that was a real talent. Singing was a skill that most beautiful women did not have but one that Whitney possessed in abundance, and she was anxious to show this talent to the world.

In 1980, she experienced what it felt like to record professionally when producer Michael Zager invited Cissy to sing on his newest album, *Life's a Party*. Cissy had taken Whitney along. The seventeen-year-old was given a solo on the album's title track and stunned everyone in the studio with her strong, seemingly perfect voice.

Zager offered her a recording contract on the spot, but Cissy turned it down. She knew how tough the music business was, and she wanted her daughter to finish school and gain a little more maturity and experience before trying it. Whitney had no say in the matter, but if she had, she would have quit school and thrown herself headlong into the world that Cissy warned her about. Ever since that Sunday morning five years ago in the New Hope Baptist Church when she had sung her first solo, she had secretly dreamed about singing professionally. This was something she *knew* she could do. But she had never crossed her strong-willed mother and she wasn't about to start now. When Cissy said no, that's exactly what she meant and none of her children dared argue with her.

Whitney fumed and bided her time. She only had a year left in high school, but she says it was the worst year of her life. Her classmates were already jealous of her status as model and cover girl, so after she sang on Zager's album and people learned about her singing talent, she was more of an outcast than ever. No way could a bunch of teenagers relate to Whitney, especially when Whitney didn't seem to want to relate to them. Her shyness had always been mistaken as aloofness, and her good looks, coupled with her regal bearing, gave the impression of arrogance.

A former classmate remembers her well. "She *did* have this attitude. She wasn't very friendly. She never went out of her way to make any friends, so she didn't have any. Even the boys left her alone. I don't remember her ever going on a date with anyone from school, so all us kids just thought she didn't like guys. Besides, she was always hanging out with Robyn Crawford even though Robyn wasn't even in school."

During her senior year Whitney continued to model because, she said, "the money was great. Where else could a kid make that kind of money for doing nothing?"

She also accompanied her mother to studio sessions, lending her voice as a background singer along with Cissy and the Sweet Inspirations. Cissy also included her daughter in her cabaret act, giving her an occasional solo number. When Whitney sang, the crowd would go wild. Even though her voice had yet to develop its full range, she seemed so beautiful standing onstage, belting out an old favorite in her big, powerful voice. Her years as a model had given her poise and self-assurance, and she played the audience like an old pro.

Friends remember seeing the young Whitney appear at Reno Sweeny's nightclub in New York where "she kicked ass. She was bad, honey. She seemed to deliberately upstage her mama—you could feel the competition between them."

Cissy graciously stepped back at those times, giving Whitney the stage, proud as any mother would be of her daughter's success, but when the song was over, it was Cissy who ruled. She never let the audience forget that it was *her* show, *she* was the star, and Whitney was just another guest singer. Soon, however, customers began calling the club to ask if Whitney would be performing that night before they made their reservations.

Cissy had worked her entire life to make it big, and now, almost overnight, her seventeen-year-old daughter was eclipsing her. Friends say Cissy was torn between jealousy and pride. Intellectually, Cissy must have known it was time to pass the baton, but she couldn't bear to see her own dream die so her daughter's could live. During this time the relationship between mother and daughter was rife with contention, but to Cissy's credit she never tried to hold Whitney back; she just wanted her to know who the *real* star of the family was.

It was hard for Whitney, attending school, modeling, and appearing in nightclubs on weekends, but she did it with a cool nonchalance that impressed everyone. She had not only inherited Cissy's singing talent but also her determination. She was tough, ambitious, and never lost sight of her goal, even if it meant giving up her senior year in high school. While her classmates were dating, going to proms, and giggling about boys, Whitney was in the studio, rehearsing. The only thing her senior year meant to her was freedom, and she couldn't wait for it to be over. Robyn was still her only friend, her staunchest supporter, and the bond between the two young women grew even stronger.

Every spare moment that Whitney had in her busy schedule,

she spent with Robyn. Both were teenagers and they needed to act like teenagers. They shopped for clothes together and often dressed identically, not caring if the other girls whispered about them behind their backs. When they walked down the street, they would hold hands or link their arms together, and they always seemed to be laughing at some secret joke they had no intention of sharing. Whitney credits Robyn's friendship as the one thing that got her through that last, miserable year, and when she graduated in 1981, she celebrated her freedom with Robyn.

Whitney had no desire to attend college. She didn't need a degree to become a star. She got her parents together (her father was still very much a part of her life) and asked their advice on how she should launch her career. Even though John hadn't had much success in managing Cissy's career, Whitney still respected him and wanted his input.

They all agreed that the young artist needed a record contract. Cissy didn't want her daughter to be exposed to the drugs and booze that were part of the crowd she would meet playing clubs. But winning a record contract wasn't easy, no matter how talented a singer might be. In the early eighties with heavy metal and new wave on the way out and disco on the way in, Whitney would have to make her own niche. Her background had been gospel, rhythm and blues, and some Broadway show tunes she had learned while appearing with the Sweet Inspirations.

So began the interviews with record executives who would be willing to give the neophyte a chance. In those days most record companies had talent scouts who went from club to club, checking out new singers and signing the most promising to contracts. It was a competitive business and Whitney had more than one nibble, but her parents held out for "the right one, the big one," who would groom her into the star they knew she could become.

Whitney continued appearing with her mother in whatever nightclub the Sweet Inspirations were booked, and Cissy always showcased her daughter, giving her several solos just in case a scout was in the audience.

Elektra Records was the first big label to show any serious interest and approached Cissy and John with an offer to sign their daughter to a recording contract. Elektra was a respected, well-known label, and the Houstons were delighted, giving their verbal agreement at once. Negotiations were quickly under way and it looked as if Whitney would soon become the professional recording star she had always dreamed of being. While managers on both sides wrangled over the fine points, Cissy and Whitney continued to fulfill their nightclub obligations.

They were performing at the Seventh Avenue South Club in Greenwich Village, playing to a packed house as usual, when word got around backstage that talent scout Gerry Griffith was in the audience. Griffith was well-known in the industry as a bird dog for the flamboyant Clive Davis, so tensions were understandably high that evening.

In the late sixties, Davis, then president of CBS Records, was personally responsible for the success of such high-profile stars as Sly and the Family Stone, Janis Joplin, Bob Dylan, Santana, and many others. It was common knowledge that he was artist oriented, willing to go that extra mile for an act he believed in. He didn't care how much company money he spent grooming and promoting new talent, and it showed in the string of hits that CBS Records enjoyed over the years.

By the midseventies, Davis had moved to Columbia Records and started his own label, Arista Records. One of his first acts as head of his own company was to sign a little-known pop singer, Barry Manilow, who had been appearing as Bette Midler's opening act in a New York bathhouse. A few months later, Manilow had become a household name. Nobody loves an overnight-success story more than young hopefuls, and soon everyone was clamoring for an audition with Clive Davis: Star Maker. To get to Davis, however, they first had to get the attention of Gerry Griffith.

That night in Greenwich Village, Whitney Houston got his attention—in a big way. He was blown away by her pure voice, her incredible beauty, her energy, and stage presence. It took him a couple of minutes before he realized who she was. He had seen her in 1980 at the Bottom Line in New York City but had not been impressed with her at the time. Now he was. In the past two years she had grown considerably as an artist, and the crowd's reaction to her convinced Griffith she was a star on the rise. He went backstage after the show and introduced himself to Whitney, telling her Arista Records would be interested in signing her. Her reaction was not what he had come to expect from young hopefuls. She gave him a haughty once-over and coolly suggested that he talk to the manager John Houston had hired for her, Eugene Harvey.

Luckily, Harvey was much more receptive to Griffith. He told him that Elektra Records had already offered Whitney a contract but it wasn't yet signed, so other options were being considered. What did Griffith have in mind? Could Arista Records offer his client a better deal than Elektra? Would Clive Davis take a personal interest in Whitney and guide her to stardom?

When Griffith approached Davis the very next morning with news of his sensational discovery, Davis merely grunted, "So show me something."

Undaunted by Davis's lack of interest, Griffith personally prepared Whitney for her audition with the "star maker." He cornered Cissy and discussed with her which songs she felt Whitney should sing. How much choreography could the teenager learn in a week's time. He even had a hand in selecting the gown Whitney would wear. The audition was to be held at Manhattan's Top Hat Rehearsal Hall, and Griffith was nervous. He was so enthusiastic about Whitney (and a little uncomfortable with his boss's lack of interest) he wanted everything to be absolutely perfect. He need not have worried. Whitney was magnificent. She performed each number with passion and youthful energy, prowling the stage like a sexy panther and sending shivers down Griffith's spine.

Davis was impressed but not nearly as enthusiastic as Griffith. He thought she had "a good voice" but she was "nothing special." He felt the best he could do was offer Whitney a singles deal, that is, one record to find out if she had "it" or not. Griffith was more than disappointed at Davis's reaction and let him know how he felt.

"This girl will be a big star, a huge star," he remembers telling Davis. "And you're going to kick yourself in the ass for not signing her when you had the chance."

Clive Davis was not an unreasonable man, and he believed in Griffith's ability to recognize star potential when he saw it, so he began discreetly checking Whitney out. He talked to his friends in the industry and learned that Whitney Houston was not just another little upstart with a big voice. She was very much in demand with other record companies. CBS Records and Elektra were both offering her long-term album contracts, and as many as a dozen smaller labels were vying for her signature. Davis quickly rethought his first offer and signed the eighteen-year-old beauty to an album contract.

Davis still wasn't bowled over by Whitney's voice, but, a shrewd businessman, he saw in Whitney a "package deal" that would appeal to a large audience. She was undeniably beautiful with a terrific body, she was the daughter of an already established and much admired performer, Cissy, the goddaughter of Aretha Franklin, and her cousin was Davis's favorite singer, Dionne Warwick. ("Dionne Warwick," Davis would say, smiling, "now *that's* a voice!")

Whitney was also a real, working model, and how many singers could claim that distinction? Her voice was strong and powerful, she had charisma, and her stage presence was impressive in one so young. To Clive Davis, Whitney Houston represented just the right mixture of clay to be molded into a superstar.

The first step would be to get her noticed, and what better way than to introduce her on national television. *The Merv Griffin Show,* hosted by Merv himself, was planning a special to honor Davis and his long career in the record business. Merv was something of a frustrated singer and would often warble a number at the opening of his show. His one claim to fame in the record business was his gigantic hit, many years before, of the novelty tune "Yes, We Have No Bananas." Sympathetic to young singers, he would often give them a spot on his show. He was a genial, laid-back host and his variety–talk show was wildly popular.

For Clive Davis to personally introduce an unknown who had yet to cut her first record sent shock waves throughout the recording industry, but that's exactly what Davis had in mind. However, if he though Whitney would be humbly grateful, as most any other unknown in her place would have been, he was mistaken.

According to Jeffery Bowman, she was flippant and cocky. "So, what's that have to do with me? He should be glad to be doing it. Hey, I'm so good, I'm gonna be great up there onstage and Clive Davis will be glad he even *knows* my ass. Should I be grateful to him? Hell, he should be grateful to me and my mother. We could be over at Elektra if he wasn't so lucky."

"It was as if she was being a little diva before her time," said an observer. "As if she *expected* royal treatment already."

Others who knew Whitney well said that she was, in fact, scared to death. Appearing on *The Merv Griffin Show* was a huge break for anyone, let alone a teenager whose career was still in the starting gate. But Whitney hid her panic behind a façade of arrogance, breezily telling everyone it was "no big deal. I'm gonna ace this gig." Just like her mother, her confidence seemed to border on conceit.

A videotape of *The Merv Griffin Show* on that long-ago day in 1983 shows a calm Whitney Houston dressed like a schoolgirl in a plain sweater and skirt. Her hair was cut as short as a boy's, but it framed her beautiful oval face to perfection, highlighting her large, almond-shaped eyes and model's cheekbones. Her first song was a ballad called "Home," and she ripped into the lyrics with such furious passion the audience was stunned. This was no shy little schoolgirl. This was a dynamo of unbridled energy and enormous talent.

The audience seemed to know they were witnessing the birth of a star, and they reacted appropriately, applauding wildly and cheering for more. Cissy then joined her daughter onstage to sing a duet of the Aretha Franklin classic "Ain't No Way," but she looked overdressed and slightly passé in her gold lamé gown and star trappings—especially standing next to the fresh-faced, simply dressed teenager who was now glowing with excitement.

Cissy must have known at that moment that her daughter was on the verge of becoming the superstar that Cissy had always dreamed *she* would be. One can only imagine the mixed emotions she must have been feeling, but in true cocky Cissy fashion she bragged to friends about *her* appearance on *The Merv Griffin Show*.

Returning to the East Coast (*The Merv Griffin Show* was done in Hollywood), Clive Davis wasted no time in setting the "star-making machine" in motion. First, he needed to find an image for Whitney. Should she be served up to the public as a sweet little teenager or a slinky diva, à la Miss Diana Ross? Whitney never used a lot of makeup—with a face like hers, she didn't need it—and she wasn't a clotheshorse, either. Perhaps she was rebelling against the days when Cissy had dressed her in starched dresses, frilly socks, and shiny Mary Janes because all during her teen years she dressed exclusively in jeans and T-shirts.

The fact that she had been a successful model still impressed Davis, and he decided on a classy, elegant look. With her tall, willowy body, haughty face, and regal carriage, he knew she could pull off "the look" with no problem. Whitney grumbled about the makeover, saying, "I just want to be myself. I don't like all that glamour stuff." Davis prevailed. Whitney was smart enough to listen to him because he was, after all, the "star maker," and she very much wanted to be a star.

By early 1984, six months before her debut album, Davis began releasing publicity photos of Whitney dressed in breathtaking gowns and elegantly coiffed wigs. Her own hair was short and nappy and she never did anything except wash and towel it dry. She would not go through the time-consuming, laborious straightening of her hair as many black women did. To her surprise, she found she liked the ease and convenience of wigs and the many different looks they afforded her. She still wears wigs today—"I don't go no place without my hair, honey"—and has dozens of them in different styles and lengths.

Davis's next move was to whet the public's appetite for her debut album. He teamed her with Teddy Pendergrass on his new album *Love Language* and pretended not to be too surprised when it shot straight up the charts to number one.

Jermaine Jackson was under contract to Arista Records at that time, and he seemed the perfect choice for Whitney's next recording. Jermaine had always been considered number three in the music industry, behind his more talented siblings Michael and Janet, and his career needed a jump start.

Davis was so delighted with the success of their "Take Good Care of My Heart" that he used it to obtain a guest appearance for both Whitney and Jermaine on the soap opera *As the World Turns.* The duo sang "Nobody Loves Me Like You Do," and Davis made sure the Hollywood gossip columnists knew about it.

He also made sure they knew about Whitney's musical heritage. Press releases during that period always identified Whitney as "the daughter of gospel and blues great Cissy Houston, cousin of the inimitable Dionne Warwick, and goddaughter of soul queen Aretha Franklin."

The hype was working, perhaps even better than Davis had predicted. The music industry was buzzing about "Clive Davis's new protégé, the beautiful Whitney Houston, now under contract to Arista Records," and record stores were suddenly getting requests for "the new Whitney Houston album"—but there was no album. Not even a single. Thus far, there had been reams of copy written about Whitney, dozens of photographs of Whitney, interviews with Whitney, gossip about Whitney—but no actual *music* by Whitney! This was a frustrating period for her. She hated the publicity, barely tolerated the interviews, and was scornful of her glamorous image. She just wanted to get into a recording studio and *sing,* but she acquiesced to Davis, admitting, "He probably knows what he's doing—I sure hope to hell he does! Shit, man, *I'm* even getting tired of hearing about me!"

4

A Rocket to Fame

IN 1980 A TELEVISION SHOW DEBUTED THAT HAD NOT ONLY THE music industry buzzing, but record buyers and music lovers as well. Called MTV, when it wasn't showing music videos, it was running nonstop commercials by the recording artists themselves, shamelessly plugging their latest releases.

It was the kind of programming America's youth could relate to and their parents could not. Flamboyant stars such as Cyndi Lauper, Boy George, Kiss, Rod Stewart, Madonna, Alice Cooper, and countless others looked straight into the camera and shouted loudly, "*I want my MTV!*" It was a great publicity stunt and it paid off in a major way. Record companies could plug their new releases without spending any money on promotion because MTV depended on free demos from the stars so as to play videos nonstop, twenty-four hours a day. It was a marriage made in marketing heaven.

By 1984, MTV had become a huge success that gobbled up new releases faster than the artists could produce them. With

VCRs in two out of every three homes, videos were the wave of the future. Adults may have covered their ears at the constant loud racket of rock and roll that blared from their youngsters' sets, but youthful consumers couldn't get enough. No longer did they have to simply sit and listen to a record. Now they could actually see their favorite rock stars gyrating onstage. It was almost as good as being at a live concert.

Clive Davis took one look at MTV and immediately knew it was the perfect showcase for Whitney. With her drop-dead good looks and polished stage presence, she would have fans lining up to buy her album. There weren't that many gorgeous black singers around. Diana Ross, while certainly stylish, could not be called beautiful in the classic sense. Nor could Aretha Franklin or Gladys Knight. Davis's favorite singer, Dionne Warwick, was a pretty woman, but even she didn't have Whitney's perfect beauty. Davis just knew in his bones that Whitney would knock 'em dead.

Making a music video was like making a minimovie, and for that Davis needed a director rather than just a record producer. Offers poured in from hundreds of video directors across the country begging for the opportunity to work with Whitney in her first video. Davis selected Michael Lindsay-Hogg, son of movie star Geraldine Fitzgerald, and shooting was soon under way.

"You Give Good Love" was the song chosen, a gentle ballad that showed off Whitney's incredible range. She sang directly into the camera, her smoky bedroom eyes caressing the lens. She moved with a lazy sensuality, and everyone in the studio had to keep reminding himself she was just an eighteen-year-old girl.

The first video was still being edited when Davis ordered the second one, "Saving All My Love for You," to be shot on location in London. This was unheard of in the music business. Whitney still didn't have an album in the stores or a song on the radio; she was simply famous for being the beautiful Whitney Houston.

When Davis ordered two more videos to be shot in quick succession, Whitney insisted one of them should be "The Greatest

Love of All," and she wanted her mother to appear with her. The song might be considered by some to be gospel because it tells of one's personal faith and belief.

It was also a song that Whitney had performed many times in Cissy's cabaret act, and she felt it would be a tribute to her mother. Not only would Whitney be publicly thanking her mother for her love and support, but also acknowledging her gospel influence. Every interview Whitney gave in those days started off with the young woman telling the reporter she "grew up in church. I was singin' gospel before I could pronounce the words."

Cissy was thrilled when she learned she would be appearing in a video, but her excitement turned to disappointment when she discovered she wouldn't be singing a note. She merely stood in the wings, smiling at her daughter as Whitney took center stage, her voice soaring like an angel's.

"How Will I Know?" was the first video that allowed Whitney to do more than just look beautiful. A choreographer was hired to teach her some kicky new dance steps, and rather than the usual sophisticated evening gowns she had worn in previous videos, she was decked out in metal mesh. Sleeveless and skintight, the dress looked as if it had been forged on her body by a blacksmith. She wore wide gold slave bracelets high up on her arms and a curly blond wig. With her café au lait complexion, soft gold gown, and honeyed hair, she looked like a statue come to life.

This was by far her most impressive video, and Clive Davis felt she was finally ready for her debut album. He had worked relentlessly for over a year and spent a quarter of a million dollars in his campaign to promote her. Some executives at Arista were a little nervous about all that cash going out and nothing coming in. They held a collective breath, hoping that Davis's gamble would pay off.

The long-awaited album hit the record stores in February 1985. "It was like a bomb went off," recalled the manager of Hits, Inc., a large record store in Hollywood. "We had barely unpacked the albums before a near riot broke out. I'd never seen so many kids in my life! The store was swarming with them, all clamoring for the Whitney Houston album. We were completely sold out in three days."

So was every other record store across America. Executives at Arista now had something else to worry about: distribution. It was like an avalanche. The more copies that were sold the more the public demanded. The media went crazy as every record reviewer across the nation sang Whitney's praises. *People* magazine gushed, "It will take an act of Congress to keep this woman from becoming a megastar." *Newsweek,* normally quite conservative, wrote, "Whitney Houston is a little frightening. No one person should have this much star quality. It doesn't seem fair."

The album, titled simply *Whitney Houston,* became the all-time bestselling debut album in music history with an unprecedented four number one hits. "You Give Good Love" was the hottest song in the world, maybe because it was the first single released from the album. No matter where I went, I would hear that song on somebody's radio or TV or stereo. And there were pictures of her everywhere—in record-store windows, in magazines and newspapers. She was the most beautiful lady I had ever seen in my life. If someone had told me then that I would one day meet her and get to know her as a close personal friend, I would have thought they were nuts.

The second half of the eighties quickly became known as the Whitney Era. In that short time she sold over 25 million records worldwide and racked up a staggering thirty awards. When Clive Davis put her on tour, every concert was sold out in advance. Her earnings were rather modest at first. She received about $15,000 per show on the first lap of her tour, but as her popularity skyrocketed, so did her income. Soon she was earning $100,000 a show, and by the end of that first year, her fee had doubled. The girl from the projects of Newark was making more money than she had ever dreamed possible.

Cissy Houston was ecstatic with her daughter's success and never passed up an opportunity to brag about her. Friends of the family said that it was obvious Cissy was reliving her own career vicariously through her daughter. She had never made it as a star on her own, so having a star daughter was the next best thing.

"Cissy basked in Whitney's limelight like a big cat stretching in the sun," one neighbor said. "The way she went on and on about record sales and concert dates and all that money, it was like it was happening to *her*. She'd praise the Lord and say things like, 'It's finally happening after all these years.' Well, she wasn't talking about Whitney because it didn't take Whitney 'all those years' to make it."

As Whitney's fame grew beyond even Cissy's lofty expectations, the young star turned more and more to her mother for guidance and refuge. "My mother is my foundation," she told reporters. It was as if she were trying to draw Cissy into her circle of fame so the older woman could experience for herself the thrill of success. And it worked. You couldn't read an article about Whitney without also reading about Cissy. Reporters inevitably wrote the same thing: "daughter of gospel and R&B great Cissy Houston."

When the National Academy of Recording Arts and Sciences announced her name among the nominees for the twenty-eighth annual Grammy Awards, in January 1986, it took Whitney completely by surprise. So much had happened so quickly, her head was still spinning and it would spin even more after all the nominees were announced to the press. Little Nippy had been nominated in three of the top categories: Album of the Year, Best Pop Vocal Performance by a Female, and Best Rhythm and Blues Solo Performance by a Female.

Everyone at Arista Records was thrilled—except Clive Davis. He was furious that his discovery had not been nominated for Best New Artist of the Year as well. His friends and associates were shocked by his ranting and raving about the imagined insult. For someone who had been in the music business as long as Davis had, he surely knew the rules of the Academy. A performer did not qualify for the New Artist category if they had a label or album credit the previous year. Whitney had received credit for both the Teddy Pendergrass and Jermaine Jackson albums.

Dionne Warwick was the presenter for Best Female Pop Performance, and when she opened the envelope and saw her little cousin's name, she let out a scream of joy. The two women hugged tightly as the huge room erupted with applause. Clutching the Grammy close to her heart, Whitney bubbled over with excitement, thanking "God and my parents, who made all this possible. I feel just like Cinderella!" Cissy and John beamed with pride. Their little Nippy was the best female singer in the whole world—and she had just told the whole world that she owed it all to them.

Even though Cissy and John had been separated for many years, they had never let their personal differences come between them and their daughter. Whitney respected their solidarity for her sake and never played favorites. She asked her father's advice as often as she asked her mother's, and she listened to what they both had to say. Regardless of his failure with Cissy's career, John Houston was still considered by many to be a good business-man—he just hadn't gotten the right breaks. He loved show business as much as his ex-wife and daughter did, and it must have galled him to work for the City of Newark while they were riding in limousines and eating at fancy restaurants. He wanted a piece of that pie for himself.

No one knows if it was with trepidation or confidence that he approached his little Nippy after the Grammies to ask her if he could comanage her career, but he did ask. Whitney didn't hesitate for even a moment. "Yes," she said. "Absolutely." Her long-time manager, Eugene Harvey, was still very much in the picture, but apparently he didn't mind sharing his superstar client. Everyone in Whitney's orbit just figured there was enough glitter to go around.

By mid 1986, Whitney's debut album had gone platinum an unheard-of six times and was still selling briskly, which caused the new Grammy winner to wonder out loud, "Who's buying it? I thought everybody in the world had one by now!"

Clive Davis didn't care who was buying it, he was just thrilled that they were. He told everyone who would listen, "Can you believe it? This kid has the all-time bestselling debut album in the entire history of music the world over!" He could not have been more proud of Whitney.

While Clive Davis was planning her second album, Whitney and her parents received an invitation from Mayor Kenneth Gibson of Newark to attend a dinner in Whitney's honor. Newark wished to show their pride in their hometown girl by giving her a key to the city. It was a glittering affair and Whitney looked the superstar in her elegant gown and understated gold jewelry. She listened graciously as Mayor Gibson gave a speech, then presented her with a plaque.

As she peered into the crowd, recognizing many people from her past, I wonder if she felt a certain smug vindication. After all, many of those young men and women in the audience had been her classmates in school. They had whispered about her, called her dirty names, and made her life miserable. If she *was* harboring any ill will, she concealed it and left the stage to a standing ovation.

By the time Clive Davis had Whitney's second album lined up, her first album was still selling briskly. Over 15 million copies were bought, and the album had stood at the top of charts for fourteen weeks. Only one other female artist, Carole King, in 1971, had had an album remain number one for that length of time, and she beat Whitney only by one week. It seemed that "number one" just automatically preceded Whitney's name in those days. Her second album came out in June 1987 and was immediately listed in Billboard's Hot 100, debuting at number one. Whitney was the only female artist ever to have an album become number one the minute it was released. Not even Madonna, who was the hottest pop star of the decade, could claim such a distinction. However, Madonna *did* top Whitney in earnings in 1987, but not by much. According to the *New York Daily News*, Madonna earned $47 million to Whitney's $44 million, both of the divas surpassing Michael Jackson's $43 million. And Whitney was just twenty-four years old.

With two bestselling albums, as well as a string of hit singles and videos, it seemed Whitney could do no wrong. The public was voracious for every scrap of information they could glean about their rock goddess. It was a slow week indeed if Whitney's photograph didn't grace some magazine cover somewhere. And the tabloids wrote about her every move. She actually knocked Princess Di off the covers of several magazines, and Oprah Winfrey was overheard saying, "Thank God for Whitney Houston! Now maybe the rag sheets will leave me alone for a while!"

Along with the praise, an equal amount of jealousy and speculation erupted. Those lesbian rumors still persisted, and Whitney did little to quiet them. When asked by reporters if there was any truth to the rumors, Whitney became either defensive or sarcastic. "*No,* I am not a lesbo," she would sniff haughtily. "Guys that say that about me are the same ones who want to jump into my pants!"

When a reported rejected her flippant answer and pursued the question, she would say that she and Robyn Crawford had been friends "closer than sisters" since their teenage years. "Even then, people thought we were gay. I think it had a lot to do with Robyn's being athletic."

However, both Whitney's and Robyn's most common response was, "If you don't understand our relationship, fuck you!" As Whitney moved up in the world, she took Robyn with her, making her "my executive assistant" as well as her longtime roommate.

The rumors persisted. There was no man in Whitney's life. She had been linked in the tabloids with a number of men, such as baseball star Darryl Strawberry, talk-show host Arsenio Hall, restaurateur Brad Johnson, the enigmatic Prince, and superstar Eddie Murphy.

Robert De Niro, whose penchant for black women is well-known, began deluging her with telephone calls and dozens of flowers, almost on a daily basis. "He'd have his home number attached," a friend said, "but Whitney wouldn't call him. She thought he was way too old for her. Then one day he sent her a teddy bear with big, gorgeous diamond earrings hanging from the ears."

Whitney did call De Niro then. She was polite but firm, telling him she was flattered but not interested. He continued to court her with flowers and gifts, telling friends he was crazy about her and just wanted a chance to plead his case in person.

Everybody in Whitney's life got into the picture with "the De Niro thing," especially Arista bigwigs, who told her it would be "career suicide" to become involved with a white man. Finally Cissy took matters into her own hands. She stuffed all the gifts from De Niro into a box with a note that read, "Return to sender. Thanks, but no thanks."

Friends and fans alike started wondering if maybe there was some truth to the gay rumors, even though Whitney continued to deny them, more angrily each time, because she was never seen with a man on a real date. She was often in the company of her brothers, Gary and Michael, or her father or some of her business associates, but never with an eligible man. She and Robyn continued to travel together and share hotel rooms, shop, and just kick back together. When reporters insisted on an answer to their question, "Is there a significant other in your life?" Whitney's angry response that she was "too busy" just fanned the flames. Surely a beautiful young woman who traveled in the circles that Whitney did would have a little free time for a dinner date.

With every magazine from the prestigious *Time* to the trashy *Globe* taking shots at her sexual preference, Whitney finally decided to talk about it with a publication she felt would understand her and not misquote her, *Rolling Stone*. She said, in part:

"I'm so sick of this shit. People want to know if there is a relationship between me and Robyn. Our relationship is that we are friends. We've been friends since we were kids. Robyn is now my employee. I'm her employer. You mean to tell me if I have a woman friend, I have to have a lesbian relationship with her? That's bullshit. There are so many female artists who have women as their confidantes, and nobody questions that. So I realize that it's like, 'Whitney Houston, she's popular, let's fuck with her.' I have denied it over and over again and nobody's accepted it."

But it was the *way* she denied it, with anger and arrogance, that continued to outrage a homophobic public. A friend of her brother Gary's told me that Whitney finally realized she would have to take some drastic steps to get rid of this stigma of lesbianism. He said she and Robyn talked and argued about it and actually had fistfights, but Whitney was stubborn. She told Robyn if the public wanted to see her with a guy, then by God she would give them what they wanted. I guess she said maybe it would be more acceptable if she was bisexual instead of gay, and she was going to start going out with guys.

Well, Robyn flipped and didn't want her going out with men, but Whitney is stubborn and she had decided that there would soon be a man in her life—and there was, Eddie Murphy. They began a much publicized love affair that delighted her fans and incensed Robyn. I heard that her affair with Eddie convinced her that maybe she was bisexual after all and just maybe men weren't as bad as she had always thought they were.

It was late 1987 when friends noticed a change in Whitney. Gone was Miss Goody Two-Shoes, the virginal young girl who gave God and her church all the credit for her success. She developed an attitude, became boastful and even more arrogant. She thought nothing of keeping concert crowds waiting for two hours or more before sauntering onstage without apologizing for her tardiness. More than once she told reporters, "I don't owe anybody anything but a good performance."

She was also rude to fellow celebrities, once showing up two hours late for a party where Boy George and Elton John were also present, then behaving boorishly and bored. According to London's *Daily Mirror*, Boy George was shocked: "What a rude cow! I've met most of the royal family, including Princess Diana. Yet, royalty wouldn't even treat people like that. She [Whitney] made me feel like a nothing."

It can be said in Whitney's defense that by this time she was completely exhausted. She had gone nonstop for the past four years, leaping from obscurity to worldwide fame faster than almost anyone else in the music business. She had been praised for her beauty and talent, screamed at by mobs of adoring fans, and pursued by packs of reporters and paparazzi.

A girl from the projects, she traveled now in limousines to four-star restaurants and elegant hotels. Her wardrobe was filled with designer clothes, and her jewels outnumbered the days of the month. She had her own personal makeup artist, hairdresser, assistants, and gofers. She had only to snap her fingers and her every wish was fulfilled.

This heady, intoxicating lifestyle would swell anyone's head—and Whitney had just turned twenty-four. Old friends who remember her said, "She never had to pay any dues like most performers who struggle for years before they achieve success. She was a teenager one day, a superstar the next."

She had been told so often and had read so often that she was the only artist in the history of music who had a debut album go platinum six times. If she believed her own press, who could blame her? Everywhere she turned, people were gushing over her, telling her how wonderful she was, how beautiful, how talented, how very exceptional.

People she had known all her life started treating her differently, with deference and even awe. Nobody called her Nippy anymore, except her father and a few relatives, she was this *goddess*, this *Miss Thing*, and it confused her and upset her. Whitney is very down-to-earth in many ways, and all the fuss both embarrassed and bored her. She still wanted to hang out in blue jeans and T-shirts, and relax with friends, but her public demanded that she look every inch the queen when she stepped out—if she *could* do so without being mobbed.

Big changes were in store for Whitney in 1988. For too long

she had listened to everyone around her, who had convinced her they knew best and she should just be a nice, quiet little girl and do what she was told. Clive Davis continued to rule her career, making all the creative decisions, her father was her manager, her mother was her personal adviser, her brothers often sang backup or traveled with her as "bodyguards." Everywhere she turned, someone was pulling at her, trying to take a piece of her, and she was tired of it. She told me once, "Who knows better than me what's best for me? *I* know what I want and I *don't* want a bunch of people in my face all the time."

In retrospect, 1988 seems to be the year Whitney rebelled in a big way. She wanted, *needed,* time alone to absorb all that had happened to her in these few short years. She told friends she wanted to explore other opportunities, maybe movies. She had been offered several scripts, including the film version of Broadway's popular *Dreamgirls,* a thinly veiled biography of Diana Ross and the Supremes. When word got around that Whitney was considering the role, Diana was furious. If a movie of *Dreamgirls* was going to be made, then *she* would play herself—not some young, brash newcomer.

When Whitney heard about Diana Ross's reaction, she supposedly laughed and said, "Then they'd have to retitle it *Dreamgrannies*—how old is she, anyway, about fifty?"

Diana Ross was nearing fifty and her star status and record sales were declining, so she was understandably hurt and insulted by Whitney's insensitive remark. She struck back, making a few scathing remarks about Whitney in the press, and Whitney retaliated by saying, "When an artist reaches a certain age, she gets a little nervous hearing the patter of little footsteps behind her. Personally, I think Diana likes the attention. I don't need the attention that bad."

Diana appeared to want to keep the feud alive in the media. She was getting more attention than she had had in quite a while. But Whitney grew bored with the speculation and announced she would rather play "a historical character—someone three-dimensional, like Josephine Baker."

This just set Miss Ross off all over again. She had wanted to play Josephine Baker in a movie since 1976, when she had performed several of Baker's songs in her concerts. She accused Whitney of making the comment just to "one up me." As it turned out, the role of Josephine Baker went to Lynn Whitfield, and both dueling divas lost out. It probably mattered a lot to Diana Ross, but Whitney simply shrugged it off in typical Whitney fashion.

5

Enter Kevin Costner
and Eddie Murphy

IN 1988, WHITNEY HOUSTON, AT TWENTY-FIVE WAS ON TOP OF THE
world. She moved to a five-acre, $10-million estate in Mendham
Township, New Jersey. Whitney seemed determined to take control of her life, to live as she wished without anyone trying to tell
her what to do—most especially, her mother. She told friends she
was tired of Cissy's constant interference and complained that she
"still treats me like a kid."

She was also annoyed by Cissy's open disapproval of Robyn
Crawford. Cissy had never liked Robyn, and now that the two
young women were older and closer than ever, Cissy couldn't
keep her mouth shut. On more than one occasion she told Whitney she had to "get rid" of Robyn or she would destroy her career, saying it wasn't "natural" for two women to be so close.

Cissy had always been strong, dominant, and formidable, but
so was Robyn—in fact, friends say of the three women, Robyn

was the most dominant. Whitney was strong, but it was easy to recognize who was the "boss" in that relationship. Robyn's job description was "personal assistant," but by 1988 she had taken charge of Whitney's career, replacing Cissy. Friends say it was Robyn who urged Whitney to take charge of her life. When Whitney bought her lavish estate and moved Robyn in, Cissy was livid. When Cissy came to visit, she was relegated to a separate guest-house, albeit a luxurious one with sauna, spa, and all the amenities. But she wanted to be in the main house with her daughter, still telling her what to do.

Regina Brown, Whitney's publicist, told me Cissy and Robyn fought over Whitney. Whitney hated being in the middle, but she wasn't about to give up Robyn for anyone, not even her mother. She retreated, hoping the two women would work it out, but they never did. If anything, Cissy's hatred of Robyn would grow stronger with the passing years.

"I think Cissy thought with me there, she'd have an alliance with Whitney," Regina told me, "because it was through Cissy that I'd gotten the job with Whitney in the first place."

Regina met Cissy in 1986 when Regina worked in Chicago for Habilative Systems, a not-for-profit organization, as a consultant for fund-raisers. She approached Cissy about doing a fund-raiser with Whitney and promised Cissy that she would do everything in her power to secure a record contract for Cissy. "I was playing her," Regina told me, "because I wanted to get to Whitney, but Cissy has such a big ego, she went for it. She *still* thinks her voice is better than anyone else in the world!"

Regina had also managed to sign Luther Vandross, and the charity fund-raiser was a huge success. She managed to get a few write-ups in newspapers for Cissy, but no record deal. "Nobody wanted to sign her," Regina said. "She was washed-up but she was the only one who didn't know it!"

That didn't faze Regina. She pursued Cissy's friendship, and at that time Cissy needed a friend to whom she could tell her troubles. She poured out her feelings about Robyn Crawford. Cissy was unhappy with Whitney's sudden display of independence and

Robyn's strong influence in her life. "She tried everything to break it up," Regina said, "but she'd finally met her match in Robyn. She was younger, stronger, and a hell of a lot more stubborn and determined than Cissy ever dreamed possible."

At Robyn's suggestion Whitney incorporated herself, starting her own company, Nippy, Inc., and that's when Cissy stepped in and tried to gain a small foothold again. She told Whitney she needed a publicity person, not for *getting* publicity but for avoiding the bad publicity she had been generating. Whitney had been booed at a recent concert, and fans were calling her a "sell-out" and "conceited" and "a diva with an attitude." Her constant tardiness at concerts as well as public functions didn't set well with people, especially since she never apologized or even bothered to offer an excuse. She would shrug and say, "Stuff happens."

"There was a lot of personal turmoil going on in Whitney's life," Regina said. "Not only was she fighting with her mother, but she was also fighting with Robyn. God, the way those two would go at it made my hair stand on end! They'd actually stand toe-to-toe and slug it out. Robyn is extremely jealous and they are both control freaks, so, man, the fur would fly! Whitney is a big flirt when she wants to be and guys were always panting after her, so were a lot of women, and this would drive Robyn up the wall. So she would retaliate by sleeping with the dancers in Whitney's group. Then Whitney would retaliate by going out on a very public date with some guy. I'm surprised those two haven't killed each other by now."

Nobody liked Robyn but everyone was intimidated by her, so they made sure they would not invite her wrath or Whitney's displeasure. A perfect example is the time Robyn *forbade* Regina to travel with Whitney to Europe, telling her, "If you go, you won't come back alive!" Regina was horrified and told Whitney what Robyn had said, but Whitney replied Regina should not worry about "Robyn's threats. They don't mean nothin', honey."

"Whitney insisted I go along on the trip, so I did," Regina told me, "but I wish to hell I hadn't. Robyn treated me like a piece of shit every chance she got. By the time we returned to the

States I could well understand Cissy's feelings for Robyn. The woman is a nutcase! She doesn't want *anyone* getting anywhere near Whitney. She's that possessive and jealous. We were all just sitting around one day—there was a roomful of people there, soon after we'd returned from Europe, and Robyn just suddenly picked a fight with me, threatening to kick my butt. She came after me with claws bared, but some of the people in the room grabbed her and held her back. I looked at Whitney and she was sitting against the wall, a smirk on her face, not saying a word. Robyn was cussing and these people were holding her arms, trying to pull her away from me, and *that's* when Whitney finally stepped in. She yelled, 'Get your fucking hands off Robyn and don't none of you ever touch her again!' Everybody hated that bitch."

Whitney's brother Michael once responded to Robyn's bad treatment of him by grabbing her by the throat and choking her before he came to his senses. "That woman is the devil in disguise," Cissy would tell anyone who would listen. "If she ever turns up dead, everybody in this office will be a suspect!"

At the 1989 Soul Train Music Awards, Whitney was nominated for and won Best Album by a Female Vocalist. As she started up the aisle toward the stage, several people in the audience booed and some yelled out, "Oreo!" Whitney was stunned and her steps faltered for a moment, then, straightening her shoulders and with a big smile on her face, she strutted onto the stage to accept the award. Although this wasn't the first time she had been booed, it hurt and surprised her that her fellow African Americans were booing. When she had learned about the nomination, she'd been thrilled, thinking that perhaps now black activists would stop saying she had sold out to the white establishment. She thought their criticism was particularly unfair as she had performed at dozens of benefits and raised millions of dollars for the United Negro College Fund as well as many other black organizations.

By the time the awards show was over, Whitney's surprise had turned to anger, and she told the waiting reporters, "They're just jealous. They've just gotten sick of me and didn't want me to win another award. No, it does not make you feel good. I don't like it and I don't appreciate it, but I just kind of write it off." By 1989, of course, she'd won so many awards she had lost count.

After accepting her award Whitney returned to her seat next to Robyn, still fuming at her humiliation when the crowd erupted in applause for the next performer. She glanced up, still angry, then straightened in her seat as the lyrics of "Don't Be Cruel," an old Elvis Presley tune, filled the huge auditorium. The guy on-stage was gyrating almost like Elvis used to and his voice was sweet and soulful. Whitney stared hard, as if to say, "Who *is* that?"

It was, of course, the bad boy of R&B, Bobby Brown, a twenty-something kid from Boston's violent, drug-wracked Orchard Park projects in the Roxbury neighborhood. Not only was he a sex symbol for every teenybopper who ever bought a record, but he was quickly becoming a huge star. He had three platinum records and a loyal following on the night he met Whitney.

Bobby Brown had first appeared on the music scene with the R&B group New Edition in the early 1980s and by age nineteen had a number one hit of his own, "My Prerogative," which firmly established him as a sex symbol with the bubble-gum generation. He was also dubbed "raunchy" when he was arrested for simulating sex onstage. Record producer Teddy Riley, who worked with Brown on a couple of his albums, told *People* magazine, "Bobby and I were both born in the 'hood and have a little bit of craziness. When I first met Whitney, I could see that she has a little craziness in her, too."

When Bobby and Whitney met the night of the Soul Train Music Awards, he didn't gush over her as most men did, which intrigued her. She wasn't used to men acting nonchalant, and she deliberately set out to win him over. She sought out Bobby after the show and invited him to a party, and even though he accepted, it was with an offhand "Why not? I've got nothin' better to do."

The booing of Whitney at the Soul Train Music Awards upset Clive Davis more than it did his headstrong star. So he began planning her third album carefully. He was tired of critics saying Whitney had a "white bread" approach to music, that she was "homogenized," and of course, the worst insult, she was an "Oreo," black on the outside, white in the middle.

Davis wanted Whitney's next album to kick some ass. He'd used the "nice, sweet, virginal little gospel singer raised in the church" publicity in the beginning, and it had worked. Now it was time to show the public that the kitten had claws. He chose mostly R&B songs and even threw in a couple of hip-hop tunes as well.

Whitney had already racked up a number of awards, including the most prestigious of all, the Grammy, two years in row, 1986 and 1987, for Best Female Pop Performance. At the 1988 American Music Awards, she had won two more awards, one for Favorite Pop/Rock Single, "I Wanna Dance With Somebody Who Loves Me." Critics had accused her of being a "crossover" into pop-rock, and if her roots were in gospel and R&B, why didn't she prove it? In between accepting awards and working on her new album, she was on the road, touring. She also worked tirelessly for several charities in an attempt to win back the favor of her African-American fans.

In February 1990, ABC paid tribute to Sammy Davis Jr., the most famous and talented black performer ever to set foot on-stage. He was in the last stages of throat cancer and would die soon after the tribute, but that star-studded night he wept openly as Whitney Houston sang "The Greatest Love of All" just for him. Sammy's longtime pal and fellow Rat Packer, Frank Sinatra, was seen wiping a tear from his eye as well. Even the elusive Michael Jackson had shown up for the event, and so had the ailing Bob Hope. It was a night no one would ever forget, especially Whitney. If she had had any doubts about being accepted by her peers, she learned that night that she was universally loved.

Whitney's third album, *I'm Your Baby Tonight,* was released in the early fall of 1990 and garnered mixed reviews, with that persistent question still hanging over her head: Is Whitney Houston black enough? Dressed in black leather and sitting astride a big, bad, black Harley-Davidson motorcycle, Whitney stared defiantly from the record cover, a slight curl to her lip, as if saying, "*Now* am I black enough?"

Whitney's longtime idol Stevie Wonder produced one of the songs on the album, "We Didn't Know," while the title song, "I'm Your Baby Tonight," was produced by Babyface and L.A. Reid, and nobody could accuse those men of being "homogenized"! The album's raw sexuality and hard edge showcased the "new, improved, grown-up" Whitney Houston. And there was another difference, too. On the first two albums, the liner notes on the back jackets thanked everyone Whitney felt had contributed to her success, producers, managers, as well as family members. She had included Robyn Crawford with her family on those first two, but on the third one, Robyn was listed as a business associate. Times were changing.

"I'm Your Baby Tonight" steadily climbed the charts in the fall of 1990 and I had heard it dozens of times. I was impressed with this "new" Whitney and had a secret fantasy of someday meeting her. My brothers and I had never given up our dream of becoming recording artists and still continued to rehearse every spare moment we had. I figured if I could get next to a big star and give them a demo of our songs, we might have a chance.

In November of that year I was working nights at the Sweetheart Cup Company as a forklift operator and during the day at my restaurant, Ammons & Lewis, and at my beauty salon, Billie Jean's. I read in the newspaper that Natalie Cole would be appearing in Chicago at the Drury Lane Theater, and I was determined to meet her and slip her a copy of my tape of the Ammons Brothers. I had the strangest feeling that something great was about to happen to me and somehow it was connected to Natalie Cole. I called the theater to ask how I could purchase some tickets, but was told it was "a private affair, not open to the public."

I should have just accepted the response but I felt that I had to go to the Drury Lane Theater. My fate seemed to depend upon it. I called back and insisted on speaking with the manager or anyone who could help me out. "I *have* to go to this performance," I told them. I guess they took pity on me because they said they would give me the name of someone who could possibly help me out. The *only* person who might do so was Regina Brown.

The phone was curtly answered, "Regina Brown speaking."

I introduced myself and was telling her what I wanted when she snapped, "Look, I don't care who you are—my cousin, my father, or the goddamn president of the United States! *Nobody* can get tickets to this show. Besides, you probably couldn't afford them anyway!"

That was like waving a red flag in front of me. I made good money and I didn't mind spending it. I kept her on the phone until she finally admitted that maybe she could get me some tickets, but they were fifty dollars each, then added sarcastically, "So, how many do you want?"

"Five," I snapped. I heard her talking to someone in the room and laughing, whispering, "This guy says he wants five tickets. Yeah, right!"

"I've changed my mind. Make that ten."

After a silence on the end of the line, she said softly, "Ten? That's five hundred dollars."

"I know how to count, lady. Now, where do I pick up the tickets?" I was furious at her rude, unprofessional behavior and planned on telling her what I thought when I saw her in person. I changed clothes, getting really duded up, then drove to the west side of Chicago to Habilative Systems. I was trying to control my temper as I paid the cashier for the tickets and asked her to point out Regina Brown.

She was sitting behind a desk across the room. She was gorgeous. She was wearing this really cute, little black velvet hat on top of shoulder-length hair, and her eyes were big and round, her complexion as smooth as silk. I walked over and held out my ten tickets and she just stared for a minute, then said, laughing, "Oh, my God—*you're* the guy on the phone!"

48

"That's right." I gave her a card from my beauty salon.

She studied it for a moment, then smiled. "Billie Jean's. From Michael Jackson's song."

"No. I named it after my little sister."

She seemed a little subdued now that she realized I wasn't just some jerk off the street, and she asked about the salon, prices and so forth, and what I thought about her hair. I removed her hat, ran my fingers through her hair, and told her she could use a touch-up. "The first visit's on me," I said. "Go ahead and call for an appointment." She did, watching me all the time she dialed, and made arrangements for ten the next morning.

I could feel something happening to me, and at the time I felt it was a premonition that my dream of becoming a recording artist was about to come true. My motive for pursuing a friendship with Regina was strictly business at this time because I felt I could get to Natalie Cole through her. I had no idea she was Whitney Houston's publicist. I will also admit that I was physically attracted to her, but I was happily married with three terrific sons and wasn't looking for anyone else.

I was at the beauty salon the next morning when Regina came in and I told her my ambitions and about the Ammons Brothers Singing Group. She said she had some heavy connections in the music business, and if I was really serious, she would be willing to listen to us and see if she could get us a spot on Natalie Cole's show. Trying to be cool, I sauntered out of Billie Jean's, then raced home and called my mother and my brothers, telling them the good news. We rehearsed all night, and the next day I closed the restaurant and we put on a show for Regina. She was blown away. Not only did she tell me how fantastic we were, but I could see her excitement on her face. She looked at me with new respect.

After she thanked everyone and promised she would let us know about the show, she looped her arm through mine and said, "Walk me to my car, baby." Once there, she threw her arms around me and kissed me—hard. I was shocked and flattered and positive that this was the beginning of my dream come true. She had given me her home phone and address so I sent a bouquet of roses and the biggest white teddy bear I could find. The moment they were delivered, she called and invited me to her place that night for dinner and cocktails. To tell you the truth, I didn't know what to expect, but no one could have kept me away. This was my date with destiny.

That night I dressed to the nines and headed downtown. I had never had reason to travel to the downtown Loop before because it was a snooty area, catering to the very rich. Regina lived on East Randolph, and as I approached her building, I noticed Mercedeses, Rolls-Royces, Porsches, and BMWs parked on the street. I was driving an Audi 5000-S, so I didn't feel too out of place as I parked it next to all the other luxury cars. Inside, however, I was a nervous wreck. Right across the street from Regina's apartment were some of the most famous hotels in Chicago—the Fairmont, Hyatt Regency, Swiss. A doorman in full regalia was standing at the entrance, and for one fleeting moment I thought he would toss me out, telling me never to come back.

As I rode the elevator to Regina's floor, my mind was in turmoil, wondering just what she had in mind. Anticipating my arrival, she stood in her doorway with a smile of welcome. She was wearing a white blouse with a thin-strapped cat suit over it that showed off every ripe curve of her body. I swallowed hard and she laughed and threw her arms around me, hugging me and pressing her body against mine.

As she pulled me inside, I noticed a wall covered with photographs of Regina with Michael Jackson, Luther Vandross, Whitney Houston—as well as Cissy and John Houston—Chicago Bears great Otis Wilson, Mike Tyson, and on and on. My mind was reeling as she laughed and said, "Everybody in the music business knows Regina Brown, honey!" That's when she told me that not only was she a close, personal friend of Whitney Houston's, but also her publicist.

All thoughts of Natalie Cole just flew from my mind. If this woman was Whitney Houston's publicist, I would try to get an introduction to *her*. She was the hottest star in the world. I can't remember saying much, I was pretty flabbergasted, but Regina chattered as she pointed out movie stars and record stars and then led me into the kitchen and produced a bottle of Piper champagne, asking me to open it.

"Careful," she cautioned, "that's the real expensive stuff, but it's the only kind I drink." I think I murmured something intelligent like, "Uh-huh," and watched as she poured two glasses half full of champagne, then filled them with orange juice. I think she called it a mimosa or something. We went to sit down on the sofa and she started firing questions at me about my group, the names and ages of the guys, what kind of experience and exposure we had had, then she surprised me by saying she wanted to manage us. *This is it,* I remember thinking, *the Ammons Brothers Singing Group are on their way straight to the top.*

We talked for hours and it was obvious she didn't want me to leave, but I had to. I was driving home when my pager went off, so I pulled over to a pay phone and called. It was Regina. "What's up?" I said. "Did I forget something?"

"Yeah," she said. "Me."

The next afternoon I was at Billie Jean's when Regina called and invited me to meet her at Hillary's for dinner; she wanted to talk some more about managing my group. She was already there when I arrived, and as soon as I sat down, she told me this was the same booth she always got when she lunched with Oprah Winfrey. She said Oprah had been wining and dining her, trying to get her to talk Whitney into appearing on her show.

"No way is Whitney *ever* going to appear on Oprah, baby," Regina said. "She doesn't like Oprah. She thinks she's a sell-out and she fawns all over the white guests, but disses the black guests. Besides, Whitney knows that Oprah would pry into her relationship with Robyn Crawford and try to put her on the spot." She laughed and shook her head. "And, baby, that *ain't ever* gonna happen!"

That was the first time I had heard Robyn's name mentioned.

In the late 1970s a draft of a screenplay called *The Bodyguard* had been floating around Hollywood. In it, a black superstar and a white security guard meet, team up professionally, and eventually fall in love. In the seventies, interracial love affairs, especially in the movies, were still taboo, so nothing much happened with the project. Then in the eighties screenwriter-director Larry Kasdan completed the screenplay and tried to get it produced. He had worked with Kevin Costner on *Silverado* and earlier in *The Big Chill,* so he first approached Costner about doing the project.

Costner was open to the idea but was in the midst of making *Dances With Wolves* and put Kasdan's script aside. Months later, after *Wolves* had been released and was acclaimed an extraordinary success (it earned over $250 million worldwide), Costner pulled out *The Bodyguard* script again and reread it. He liked the controversial theme, the danger of taking a chance with an interracial love affair, and he decided to do it. He needed something big and ballsy to follow his first flush of success as actor-director, and he wanted a project that would make the public take notice. He didn't want anyone to think that *Dances* was just a fluke.

With cash registers still ringing in the background and every major studio in Hollywood clamoring to get Costner's next project, he could afford to pick and choose. It's been rumored that his handlers tried to talk him out of it, telling him that middle America, namely the Bible Belt, wouldn't accept a black-white relationship, no matter how big the star was. But Costner was adamant. He wanted to do *The Bodyguard,* and in 1990 whatever Kevin wanted, Kevin got.

Now came the problem of casting the black superstar who was described in Kasdan's script as young, gorgeous, sexy, and bitchy. Several lovely black actresses could have played the part, but Costner wanted a *real* singer. Every time anyone wanted a black actress who could sing, or vice versa, they called on Diana Ross. She had proven her acting talent in *Lady Sings the Blues* and everyone knew she could sing, but there was one big problem. Diana was ten years older than Costner.

It didn't take a rocket scientist to figure out that Whitney Houston was young, black, gorgeous, sexy, *and* bitchy! Costner had never met her, but he, along with millions of other fans, had certainly seen her videos, and he thought she would be perfect for the part. But could she act? Many singing stars had tried to make the transition from singer to actor and had failed. Latest case in point: Madonna. (As crazy as it sounds, some big wigs at Warner Bros. had tried to convince Costner to hire Madonna for the role. He reportedly said, "Hey, fellas, the last time I looked, Madonna was white!")

Costner personally called Whitney and asked her if she would like to star in his next movie, but the diva appeared unimpressed and said she would get back to him. She wasn't unimpressed, however, and told Regina that she had almost had a heart attack when she heard Costner's voice on the phone. He was the biggest star in show business in 1990, and he was also handsome, shy, and personable. A killer combination, but Whitney's natural skepticism made her check it out. When her agent came back with the good news, "Yes, the offer is legitimate," she immediately agreed without even reading the script.

There was just one snag—Costner would have to wait until Whitney completed her concert tour. Her third album had just appeared and she was booked for a full year. No problem, Costner would wait. "I just had a gut feeling about her," he said.

I'm Your Baby Tonight went double platinum, and the title single reached number one. This was Whitney's eighth number one song and she had now tied the record set by Madonna. She had also found the time for a little romance in her life, and she renewed her relationship with Eddie Murphy. This time it was definitely a sexual relationship, not the old "we're just friends" story she had told the media in the past. The tabloids couldn't get enough of this pairing and wrote about them constantly. Two of the most successful and good-looking black stars in show business were billing and cooing all over town, and the paparazzi had a field day.

"Robyn was livid," Regina told me. "Absolutely *incensed* and ordered Whitney to stop seeing him, to stop making a fool of herself over this guy, this mere *man!* Robyn really hates men."

But Whitney defied her. Maybe she was finally beginning to appreciate the perks of being able to date openly, to go out in public with someone she cared about without having to answer to a bunch of critics about her sexual preference.

6

Whitney's Troubles

WHILE MY BROTHERS AND I WERE REHEARSING FOR OUR APPEAR-ance at the Drury Lane Theater, Regina continued to call me four or five times a day and invite me out. I was spending several nights a week at her apartment, having dinner with her, drinking champagne, and talking until dawn. The conversations usually started out with plans on how she would help my career, but after a few bottles of champagne we would end up in these wild necking sessions.

I was usually the one to put a stop to it and say I had to go home. I loved my wife, Marsha, and had always honored my marriage vows, so to find myself kissing and groping this other woman made me feel pretty guilty. I had always worked nights, so it wasn't difficult to explain to Marsha where I'd been. She just assumed I was at work.

Every time I was at Regina's she would get a lot of phone calls from Cissy or Whitney. From Regina's side of the conversation it was obvious Cissy was either complaining about Whitney or Robyn. And when Whitney called, she would be complaining about everything. She said she was so damn unhappy, so tired of all the media attention, of being on the road. She wanted to settle down, take a breath, and have some time to enjoy all the money she had made. She would be on the phone with Regina for hours at a time while I was sitting there listening.

"She's a very troubled young woman," Regina told me. "She wants a normal life but she also wants to be a superstar. She's got this thing going with Robyn Crawford, but she wants children and a family. On one hand, she's as tough as nails, but she allows both Robyn and Cissy to push her around. Maybe that's why she's starting to push other people around now, to have some sort of control in her life. I just know she's got some major problems and she's going to have to deal with them before she ever finds happiness."

Even though her new album had already gone platinum twice and her concerts were sold-out, critics continued to snipe at her. They compared her debut album to this latest one and reported that "sales were disappointing," and some claimed she shouldn't have tried to "go hard," they liked her better when she was homogenized." Oddly enough, they were the same critics who had blasted her in the past for being "too homogenized."

"There's no pleasing them [the media]," Whitney said. "They're devils to me. They're out to eat my flesh."

"She just simply doesn't know how to handle the press," Regina said. "She's flippant and snotty and looks down her nose at reporters, and she's *always* late, at least an hour, sometimes two hours. She struts in surrounded by a nearly impenetrable entourage of bodyguards and assistants. Then she wonders why they label her a diva."

Regina had told me the Ammons Brothers Singing Group would do four songs that night at the Drury Lane Theater. We pooled our money and bought custom-made designer suits and we were ready. We had also bought a table right next to the stage for our friends and family. When we arrived, we discovered that

Regina had resold our table. I was furious but she was unfazed and scurried about trying to find another table. We had to split up and I found myself sitting at the bar in the back of the room. I was embarrassed because I'd told my family this was my big night. Then came the next blow.

"I'm *sooo* sorry, baby," Regina said sweetly, pressing herself against me. "But you guys are only going to have time for one song tonight." She gave some vague explanation about schedules and other things, but the bottom line was "one song"—after we'd worked so hard. I was livid but I held my temper. This could still be my chance and I wasn't about to blow it.

People were eating dinner before Natalie Cole and the other stars came on, so the Ammons Brothers Singing Group turned out to be the opening act. A kind of warm-up before the "real" show started. I'm not even sure they heard us, there was so much noise with silverware clanking and people talking and waiters running around. Natalie Cole wasn't even watching us. She was in her dressing room eating dinner. Also, another band was setting up right behind the curtain as we were singing. I'd never been so humiliated in my life.

As I sat with my mother trying to explain to her what had happened, Regina came sashaying over. She was wearing a lime green suede suit and looked terrific. She made a big fuss over my mother, then grabbed my hand and pulled me onto the dance floor. It was hard to stay mad at her when she was turning on the charm, especially when she was whispering in my ear, telling me how fabulous I looked and moaning that she wanted to make love to me right then and there. She was rubbing against me, kissing me long and deep on the mouth. Every so often I got a glimpse of my mother's face, and she was shocked. I didn't know what to do. By this time I knew that Regina was a master of manipulation and that she lied even when the truth would serve her better, but I was hooked. I wanted her as badly as she said she wanted me. We still hadn't made love, even though by now I was certainly more than ready and willing.

While Regina was out of town for a couple of days, I did a

lot of thinking about our relationship. I decided that if I was going to continue seeing her, I would tell her about my wife and kids. She called to apologize for not getting in touch with me sooner but said she had been with Cissy day and night. Then she asked me if I was sitting down because she had something to tell me.

"I've never wanted to be with a man as badly as I want to be with you, Kevin," she said. "I've dreamed about making love to you a thousand times, but I'm afraid you won't want me after you see my body." She then explained, in gory detail, every single thing that had happened to her during breast cancer surgery. Not only had the doctors fashioned new nipples from flesh taken from her vagina, but they had also removed bones from her rib cage to support her stomach wall. She said she was a mass of scars and had "a body from hell," and she couldn't stand looking in the mirror, so she could just imagine what I would think. She said the surgery had left her so devastated and with such low self-esteem she had even considered suicide.

"Then I met you," she said, "and I started feeling like a woman again, but I had to explain everything so you'd know what you were getting into."

I was shocked but I also felt admiration for her—and I still wanted her. I told her, "It'll take more than that to chase me away. When you get home, I'll prove it."

She was almost crying when she said, "Thank you, Kevin, you'll never know what you've done for me." She said she'd be home Friday, and it was longest three days in my life.

I had four dozen roses and several cards delivered to her apartment on her arrival, and she called me at once, crying and laughing, and asked me to come over. She couldn't wait to see me.

We went to Pops For Champagne, a romantic little restaurant with live jazz and great food, then went back to her place. We fell into one another's arms the minute the door closed behind us, kissing madly, and she kept saying, "Are you sure, Kevin? Are you sure, baby?"

"I'm sure," I said, "I'm sure, Regina. It's okay, baby." I sat on the sofa while she went to change, and when she came out of the bathroom wearing a thin white robe, I wondered if it really would be okay. I hoped I could handle it and that my expression wouldn't betray any shock or revulsion. She stood in front of me and dropped the robe, and I *was* shocked. She'd been right, her body was covered in scars and it took me a few seconds to recover. I took her in my arms and she started crying and so did I. We just held on to each other, crying, then we kissed and everything was suddenly all right. I no longer saw the scars. I saw a beautiful, desirable woman with such pure love shining from her eyes that it staggered me.

Later, when we were lying in bed together, I noticed a picture on her nightstand of her and Michael Jackson, and they were kissing. *That's a collector's item,* I thought, *Michael kissing a woman.* She jumped out of bed, returning with a photo album filled with pictures of Michael, Whitney, Robyn, and herself. She said they were taken at Michael's house, and there was a cozy one of Whitney and Robyn in a carriage. She said the only way to get to Michael's Never Land ranch was by helicopter, and then she told me a story that made me shudder. She said one time Whitney had gone to the ranch with Robyn to present Michael with some award, and suddenly, right before her eyes, his cheeks started slipping.

"He'd had implants to give him high cheekbones, and they just came loose and slipped right down his face, resting on his jaw." Regina was laughing and rolling all over the bed. She showed me more pictures of celebrities, and when I saw one with her and Luther Vandross looking real chummy, I asked if she'd ever had an affair with him.

She laughed and rolled her eyes. "Not hardly, honey. I'm not his type."

I had yet to learn a lot about Regina, but that night nothing mattered because I realized I'd fallen in love with her. The next day she paged me at least twenty-five times, and every time I called her back she said the same thing: "I was just thinking about you. I love you, Kevin Ammons."

A couple of weeks later at Regina's I saw a tabloid on the coffee table with a big, bold headline: "Whitney Houston Pregnant With Eddie Murphy's Baby!" I scanned it quickly: "Whitney Houston and Eddie Murphy are getting married this spring. And if that's not enough to quell the rumors of Houston's sexual preference for women, Murphy is tying the knot because she's pregnant with his child."

"Everybody's always saying that Whitney only dates Eddie to stop the rumors that she's gay and really having an affair with Robyn," Regina said. "But she's crazy about Eddie. I just wonder if he feels the same way about her."

News that a war was brewing in the Persian Gulf pushed Eddie and Whitney off the front pages as Americans rallied to show their support for President Bush and their patriotism. This was January 1991, and with the Super Bowl coming up, organizers needed somebody extraspecial to sing the national anthem. Who better than America's most popular diva, Whitney Houston?

Clive Davis was ecstatic. His client would be performing before a television audience of over 100 million viewers, and he planned to capitalize on it. Even though "The Star-Spangled Banner" would be performed live, Davis brought in a truckload of sophisticated electronic equipment to make sure he had a release-quality tape of Whitney's voice. Davis realized that to make a killing off Whitney's recording he had to keep his plan secret until after the Super Bowl, so what the audience saw wasn't exactly what they were getting. They didn't know Whitney was being recorded as she stood in front of them, both hands gripping the mike as she belted out the familiar lyrics. Her voice was never stronger or purer as it soared with emotion. She was riveting, stunning, and in that one moment she captured America's heart. Patriotism was high as our boys and girls prepared to go to war, and Davis wanted to make sure they left with the sound of Whitney's rendition of the national anthem in their hearts and minds.

Whitney didn't let Davis down—she wowed the world and had every reporter with a computer singing her praises. Said the *New York Times:* "A full orchestra accompanies Ms. Houston's sinuous, sultry voice, which makes the national anthem voluptuous; under the last note is the whoosh of F-16 jets flying overhead."

With that one song, Whitney had managed to turn public opinion back in her favor. She couldn't be all that bad, critics reasoned, if she could put such heartfelt passion into our national anthem. Davis announced his company, Arista, planned to send free copies of the recording to the servicemen and servicewomen in the Gulf. When pressed by fans to release it in the States as well, Davis acted as if it were a hell of an idea and why hadn't he thought of it? However, some reporters discovered that Davis had made elaborate plans for a recording *before* the Super Bowl, and they asked, was he exploiting the war to make a fortune on the Super Bowl appearance?

"Not at all," Davis huffed, then promised that all profits from the single and the video would be donated to a war-relief charity "to be chosen by Ms. Houston." He was an American and every bit as patriotic as the next guy.

He made good on his promise, donating over half a million dollars to the American Red Cross Gulf Crisis Fund as well as the Whitney Houston Foundation for Children. That this patriotic act of charity also reaped enormous publicity for Whitney and her new album was just a coincidence. When the single was released, "The Star-Spangled Banner" was on one side, "America the Beautiful" on the other. It went straight to number one on the charts. The only other time in history that this had happened was with Kate Smith's recording of "America the Beautiful," some forty years earlier.

Critics and fans alike were stunned by the success of this single, and Whitney's popularity hit an all-time high. It was almost like the very beginning of her career when she could do no wrong. Whitney Houston was so good she could get a hit record from a song that had been written in 1814—176 years ago!

61

"She may have been America's sweetheart," Regina told me later, "but you should have been at the Super Bowl. You wouldn't believe what a knock-down-drag-out went on between her, Robyn, and Cissy." I pressed her for details and she said:

"M.C. Hammer showed up with his entourage and he and Whitney were off by themselves, talking, laughing, being real friendly, and Robyn flipped. When they were leaving the skybox, Robyn grabbed Whitney's arm and pulled her aside and started giving her a ration of shit about flirting with Hammer. She was really pissed off that Whitney was suddenly dating all these *guys* and trying to make people think she wasn't with Robyn anymore. I guess a couple of days before that, Bobby Brown had sent Whitney four hundred roses, and Robyn was seething with jealousy. I heard her yell something about Whitney better not ever dis her that way again, and Whitney jerked away and said, 'Go to hell!'

"With that, Robyn hauls off and slaps Whitney's face. There was a bunch of people standing around and they were all just staring, but instead of fighting back, Whitney broke into tears and ran away. I followed her and we were getting our stuff together, ready to leave, when we heard this commotion. Cissy was confronting Robyn and she was breathing fire and yelled, 'What the fuck did you put your hands on my baby for?' Then—wham!—she slugs her right in the jaw with her fist! Then she hits her again and Robyn fell to the ground, but Cissy kept on punching her and kicking her, yelling, 'I'll kill you, you stupid ass bitch!'

"Onlookers broke up the fight, pulling Cissy off Robyn, and I hustled Whitney out of there and back to our hotel room. She was crying and everything and we talked for about two hours, with me trying to calm her down. The phone kept ringing but Whitney told me not to answer it. Then the door burst open and Robyn rushed in, crying hysterically and telling Whitney how sorry she was and she kept saying over and over, 'I love you, baby, I just love you too much!' Whitney pulled her into her arms and they started kissing and crying, and I very discreetly turned off the lights and left the room."

Regina told me that one of the conditions of working for Whitney was that you never said a word about Robyn to anyone. To insure her silence, Whitney had given Regina many expensive presents: a gold Mercedes-Benz, a diamond-studded cross, a corporate card, a calling-card account, diamond earrings, free airplane travel, $125,000-a-year salary, and free rent on her luxurious apartment.

My affair with Regina had really heated up by this time, and I was spending almost every night with her. One night we were lying in bed at about 3:30 A.M. when the phone rang. She answered it, saying, "Hi, Nippy. What's up?"

After she hung up, she told me Whitney had asked her what she was doing awake at that hour; she must be doing "the wild thing" and wanted to know who with.

"I had to get me some," Regina said, laughing, looking over at me. "Kevin is a stubborn ass but I truly love him. . . . Okay, I'll introduce you guys next time we get together. You'll like him."

Whitney told Regina she'd called to let her know she would be receiving a package from Federal Express the next morning, and Whitney wanted to make sure that everything went as planned.

I was still there when the package arrived and watched Regina open it. It contained photographs of Whitney and Randall Cunningham, quarterback for the Philadelphia Eagles, taken by Whitney's photographer, Marc Murphy Bryant. Regina had been instructed to sell them to the tabloids or "give them away free," Whitney told her. "I don't care what you do, just get them in the rags."

Whitney was still carrying a torch for Eddie Murphy, and she wanted to get back at him for dumping her. She thought if he saw her with other guys, he would become jealous and come back to her. Whitney had a brief fling with Randall at her place in Antigua and he was hooked, telling Regina that he was in love with Whitney. He would call and Regina would put him on the speakerphone so I could listen. The guy sounded upset and couldn't understand why Whitney wouldn't talk to him. He would plead with Regina to have Whitney call him back, and Regina would promise him Whitney would—then she'd roll her eyes at me and say, "He's such a nerd."

Regina called Whitney and told her the photographs had just arrived, and Whitney said to give them to the rags but make sure no one knew they came from Nippy, Inc. So Regina asked me if I would submit them to the tabloids since nobody would connect me with Whitney. I agreed but told her instead of giving them away, why not sell them? The *Enquirer* and *Star* and the *Globe* would pay big bucks for them.

"I'll tell you what, baby," she said. "If you can sell them, you can have the money."

On my way home, I stopped at the Jewel food store and bought a copy of every tabloid they had, then put together a story line to accompany the pictures. I called all the editors, leaving a message saying I was Whitney Houston's bodyguard and I had exclusive photos of her and a new secret love, Randall Cunningham, and would be willing to sell them. Within an hour, my phone was ringing off the hook. I told them I wanted $20,000 and they said this was not a problem, as long as I had the negatives. England's *Sunday Mirror* of London said they would send a courier to meet with me and verify the photos.

I called Regina with the news. She was thrilled but told me she had to talk to someone and would call me right back. She did but it was a three-way conversation with somebody named Simone, and Regina told me to explain everything—what I had told the newspaper, their telephone number, etc.—that Simone was a good negotiator and she would take over.

I was furious. I had made all the calls and come up with a solid, believable story, so I wasn't about to let someone else take the credit. I told Regina as much and was ready to drop out when she apologized and said, "No, no, baby, that's okay. You handle the deal."

I arranged to meet the courier across the street from Regina's apartment at the Fairmont Hotel, and I insisted that she accompany me. She didn't want to be seen in case they could connect her to Whitney, so she waited in my car while I went inside to talk to the guy.

As soon as I walked into the lobby, this fellow came forward, extending his hand. "Are you Kevin Ammons?" he asked in a British accent. I said I was and we got down to business. I gave him the photos and negatives. He pulled out this loop and studied each one, then asked me to tell him again how I had obtained them. I said I was Whitney Houston's bodyguard and I had gotten the pictures and I wanted to sell them: "Just let me know if you're interested." He said he was, but the paper could only pay ten thousand, not twenty. When I had asked twenty, I was expecting that they'd come back with an offer of ten or fifteen.

I told him I would have to check with my "wife," who was outside in the car, and would be right back. I was thrilled and leaned in through the car window to give Regina a big kiss, telling her I'd done it; we had ten big ones waiting for us. To my total surprise and shock, she said, "That dude's full of shit, man! He probably doesn't even work for a newspaper and just wants to get his hands on the pictures so he can sell them for fifty thousand! What's his name, anyway?" I told her and she said, "Fuck him. I'll give them away before I let that motherfucker take advantage of you."

I told her I didn't need this kind of shit. "Now get the hell out of my car; I have to go to work."

The next morning she called me, apologizing, sweet-talking me, and told me she had decided she was just going to send the pictures back to Whitney. She didn't want something as stupid as this to come between us. I was mollified and everything went back to normal until two weeks later when I received a phone call from the editor of the *Sunday Mirror,* calling from London. He wanted to know if there was any truth to the rumor that a romance was brewing between Whitney and Bobby Brown. He said he would be willing to pay me much more than he had paid for the Randall Cunningham story. It took me a second to figure out what must have happened, but I calmly asked if he'd fax me a copy of the story since I hadn't seen it.

I stuffed the copy of the fax in my pocket and drove to Regina's. She was surprised to see me but asked me in and I said, "Is there something you want to tell me?"

"What do you mean?" she asked, genuinely puzzled. It had never occurred to her that I would find out about the story because the *Sunday Mirror* was published in London.

I kept my cool and asked again, "Regina, are you sure there's not something you want to tell me?"

She shook her head, frowning. "No. I don't know what you mean."

"That's very interesting. I just got a call from the editor of the *Sunday Mirror*, and he thanked me for allowing my 'wife' to sell them the Whitney Houston story."

She jumped up and yelled, "He's a fucking liar! I didn't sell any damn story to anybody."

"Sit down before I knock you down." I picked up the phone and pretended to place a call to London.

"Hang up the phone, baby," Regina said, and started crying. She did her sweet-talking number with me again and apologized for lying to me. She said she had split the money with her aunt and with Whitney's godmother, Ellen (Aunt Bey) White, because she didn't think I needed it as much as they did. The check had been made out to Evette Bassette, Regina's assistant, and she'd also given Simone a thousand bucks. She was crying and hanging on to my hand, then started to kiss me and pulled me into the bedroom and made it all better the only way she knew how.

I know I should have walked out then, but I was in love with her. Also, I didn't want to blow what I thought would be my chance at a singing career. She had told me hundreds of times that she had told Whitney all about me, and just as soon as Whitney had some spare time, she wanted to hear the Ammons Brothers Singing Group. She said Whitney could get me a contract with Arista Records because she kept them alive and they owed her big time.

A couple of days later I was in the apartment alone. Regina had gone to the market and I answered the phone and heard this familiar voice asking to speak to Regina. I recognized Whitney at once and said Regina was out, but I'd be glad to take a message.

"This must be Kevin," she said. "I've heard a lot about you and I can't wait to meet you." Her voice sounded throaty and sexy, a little hoarse. Regina had told me several times that Whitney smoked so much pot laced with cocaine that she was developing polyps in her throat and had been warned by her doctor to stop. I'd been around pot smokers and dopers all my life and I recognized that hoarseness immediately. But I wasn't thinking about that at the time; I was so thrilled to be talking to Whitney Houston.

This was March 1991, and Whitney was scheduled to perform at a special concert for the troops who were returning from the Gulf. It would be an HBO special called "Welcome Home, Heroes" and would be held at the Norfolk Naval Station in Virginia on the thirty-first. Whitney told Regina to invite me. At first, Whitney wasn't too thrilled to do the show, but they offered her "millions of dollars," Regina said, and Whitney changed her mind. Regina told me that Whitney was under a lot of pressure because Robyn was giving her grief about Bobby Brown. Also, her father, John Houston, had run off with Whitney's maid, twenty-nine-year-old Barbara Peggy Griffith from Trinidad. Whitney was livid and fired the woman on the spot. She refused to speak to her father and told Regina, "He's old enough to be Peggy's grandfather, for God's sake!"

Regina would put Whitney on the speakerphone and would listen to her crying. She seemed so miserable and lonely. Regina would tell her she should get rid of Robyn, find a nice guy, and have some kids. Regina was patient with her, listening to her for hours, soothing her and calming her down, telling her that everything would be okay.

7

A Tough Broad

I ARRIVED IN NORFORK, VIRGINIA, ON MARCH 30, A CHILLY, RAINY day. Regina had gone there a few days earlier to be with Whitney while she rehearsed. Regina was waiting for me at the airport. She came flying across the room and literally jumped into my arms hugging and kissing me. A limousine driver was with her, and he picked up my luggage and I just automatically offered to help. I was used to carrying my own bags, but Regina snapped, "That's his job, not yours!"

We pulled up in front of the Omni Hotel. Dozens of teen-agers were milling about on the sidewalk holding signs and pictures of the group New Kids on the Block. Regina said they were also appearing in Norfork and were staying on the same floor as we were.

The next day we went to a mall and did some shopping before we met Whitney. I was a nervous wreck. I had wanted to meet her for so long. I had heard her on the speakerphone countless times, pouring out her heart to Regina. According to Regina, Whitney was interested in hearing my singing group and had told

69

her she couldn't wait to meet me. Regina had laid so many stories on me that I wasn't sure she was telling me the truth, but I believed her because I *wanted* to believe her so badly. All my life I'd dreamed of being a star, and I just knew that if anyone could help me realize that dream, it would be Whitney Houston.

Whitney was doing a sound check when Regina and I walked in, and I was bowled over at how beautiful she was in person. Every picture I'd ever seen of her was stunning, of course, but none of them did justice to her incredible skin. Her eyes danced with intelligence and mischief as she looked at me and said, "So this is the Kevin I've heard so much about. It's a pleasure to finally meet you."

"The pleasure is all mine," I assured her.

I also met Robyn Crawford, whom I'd heard so much about. She was wearing a man's double-breasted suit and men's shoes. Her hair was cut in a short crew, military style, and she wasn't wearing any makeup. Her face was pretty with fine features, but she looked grim and unfriendly and hardly ever took her eyes off Whitney. She gave me a quick once-over, her expression hard, then dismissed me.

We watched the rehearsal, then left to have dinner, and all the time Regina was chattering away, my mind was on Whitney. I'd never seen a body like hers. It was both slender and willowy and yet voluptuous and sensual.

When we arrived for the show that evening, Michael Houston asked me if I'd sit next to his mother, Cissy, and keep an eye on her. She had a cast on one leg and he was afraid an overly zealous fan might bump into her. So there I was, front row center, when Whitney swept onstage. She was dazzling. Her skin, her hair, her smile—everything about her glowed as if she'd been lit from inside.

The audience of over three thousand people, mostly Gulf veterans and their families, whistled and stomped, giving her a standing ovation. She squared her shoulders, grabbed the mike, and in a strong, pure, powerful voice, belted out the national anthem—a cappella. It was as if she were thumbing her nose at the critics who had taken potshots at her for recording the song at the Super Bowl.

The show was spectacular, and at one point, Whitney reached down to the first row and plucked a baby off the lap of a serviceman. She sat the kid on a stool, singing to him, and he was weaving around; he was too young to sit up on that high stool by himself. To this day I don't know what ever possessed me to take matters into my own hands, but I stooped in front of the stage and told Whitney to take the baby off the stool and return him to his father. When I sat down next to Cissy, I explained that I was afraid the child would fall off. He wasn't old enough to sit by himself and Whitney might be sued.

Cissy said she hadn't thought of that and thanked me and gave my hand a little squeeze. People were bringing bouquets of roses to Whitney, and I wondered why the security people hadn't intercepted the flowers to see if they contained anything harmful. I know it may sound paranoid, but a lot of sick people are out there. All it takes is one nutcase who wants to get his name in the paper for killing a celebrity.

After the show I apologized to Whitney for suggesting that she take the baby off the stool and explained why I'd done it. She was grateful and thanked me for my interest. I also mentioned that she shouldn't take flowers directly from fans, she should have her security men check them first. "You never know when some crazy asshole might have a pistol hidden in the bouquet, ready to blow you away," I said, and her eyes widened in fear. Every big star is somewhat afraid when they mingle in crowds, and Whitney was no exception. Also, she had received a lot of bad press in the past couple of years and was understandably wary.

Regina hissed at me, "Knock it off, Kevin. It's not your place to watch after Whitney."

But Whitney was grateful and told me so. I heard later that heads had rolled because her security people hadn't done their job.

The next morning Whitney was invited to be guest of honor at a brunch given by the executives of HBO to show their appreciation and to say thanks for her sensational performance. Her family and friends were also invited. I sat next to Regina, Cissy and John Houston, and Whitney's gofer, Sylvia. John was trying to be cozy with Cissy, pretending they were still a happily married couple, and every time he leaned in close to talk to her, I saw a look of pure hatred spread over Cissy's face. She was still humiliated by his affair with Peggy Griffith and the fact that she was a maid, for God's sake! And her own daughter's maid at that.

Cissy knew people were whispering behind her back and feeling sorry for her, and she couldn't stand that. She also knew that friends and relatives were laughing at how ridiculous it looked, a seventy-year-old man and a twenty-nine-year-old woman. Peggy was younger than his two sons and just one year older than Whitney. It made Cissy feel like a fool, and nobody got away with making Cissy Houston look the fool.

I saw her pick up a fork from the table and turn to face John. Her teeth were clenched, her expression filled with venom. "Get the fuck away from me," she hissed, "or I'm gonna stick this fork right in your eye!"

John quickly moved back from the table, then one of the executives from HBO took his arm and asked him when Whitney was coming down. The executive said his wife was one of Whitney's biggest fans and was dying to meet her. We had already been waiting for close to an hour, and everyone at the table was getting restless. John motioned Sylvia over and asked her to call Whitney's room and let her know that everyone was waiting for her.

The look on Sylvia's face could only be described as sheer terror and dread. Everyone who worked for Whitney knew she would take your head off if you dared disturb her before three in the afternoon. Reluctantly, Sylvia made the call from a house phone, and I learned later that Robyn answered and immediately began cussing and screaming for being awakened so "goddamned early." Sylvia told her she was calling for John and that everyone was waiting to eat until Whitney came down. At that point Whitney got on the phone and told Sylvia to listen carefully and to "tell my father exactly what I say, word for word, don't change a thing, you got that?"

I was watching Sylvia's face and she probably wished she was anywhere else in the world except in the dining room of the Omni Hotel. She just stood by John's chair, her head down, and told him, "Whitney's not coming down. She said HBO paid her to perform, not to have breakfast with them. And if anybody has a problem with that, it's too fucking bad!"

Needless to say, the atmosphere at the table changed and everyone pretty much talked among themselves until breakfast was over. Regina went back to our room and I went over to talk to John. He looked pretty miserable standing there all by himself, and as soon as I approached, he started cussing.

Instead of being mad at Whitney for humiliating him, he tore into the HBO executives. "Just look at all these white motherfuckers waiting to meet my little girl. They don't give a shit about her or anyone else for that matter. The only thing they care about is using her to make money for them."

He was seething with rage, and it was more than just the fiasco in the dining room. This man had some really deep anger inside him. "White motherfuckers have always used us black folks," he snarled. "I'd like to drop a bomb on the whole worthless lot of them."

As I got to know him better over the next few years, I realized that his anger stemmed from his failure as a music promoter and manager. He had wanted stardom for Cissy not just for her but for himself. He fancied himself another Berry Gordy, Clive Davis, or Quincy Jones, and when it didn't happen, he became bitter and resentful. One thing about the Houstons, they've all got more ego than anyone else I've ever met.

The next day I took a lot of pictures of everyone connected with the show as well as some of me and Whitney. I couldn't wait to tell my family all about my trip and show them pictures of me hobnobbing with Whitney Houston. She was warm and friendly to me, draping her arm around my shoulders and smiling right into my eyes. Once I overheard her say to Robyn, "He's a big one, isn't he? Maybe I should hire him as my bodyguard."

When I got home and unpacked, I found that my roll of film was gone. That could only mean one thing: Regina. She didn't want me to have pictures of Whitney and me together. I asked her about it and she said she'd dropped my film off along with hers at a Walgreen and she would pick it up when it was ready. I had used her camera but bought my own film, so I guess that made sense. I asked about the film several times over the next three weeks, and she kept telling me it wasn't ready yet. I knew she was lying so the next time I was at her place I looked around and found my film hidden in the bottom of her bathroom cabinet. It didn't do her any good. I just took it back and had several copies made.

Once I had met Whitney and her family, I was included in most of their activities. Michael and I became good friends and would often relax together, smoking weed, bullshitting about women. His half brother, Gary Garland, was often around, too, but I didn't like him as much as I did Michael. One day the three of us decided to go to the gym and shoot some hoops, but before we left we were sitting in my house, smoking weed and drinking a few beers. Michael pulled this packet out of his pocket and asked if I had any baking soda and could he borrow a spoon. I grew up in the projects and knew the ritual for smoking cocaine. They offered me some but I passed. I only smoked weed.

After I drove them back to their hotel, I decided to go up to their room with them for another joint. Just as we entered the lobby, we saw Whitney and Cissy coming out of the bar, and one look at Whitney's face told us she was furious. She stomped up to Michael and said, "Where the fuck have you been and why didn't you tell me where you were going?"

"We were at the gym," Michael said. "I told Regina where we'd be."

"I don't give a fuck," Whitney yelled. "You answer to me. If you ever pull this shit again, you won't be working for me!"

"So fire me then," Michael yelled back, just as angry as his sister. They both had volatile tempers, and the least little thing would set them off. He turned away, saying, "Fuck you, Whitney," and she slapped him hard across the face.

"You bitch," Michael yelled, and slugged her in the face with his fist—and she slugged him right back with her fist! They were standing toe-to-toe throwing punches like a couple of men, and Cissy was just watching.

After they had exchanged a couple of more blows, Cissy stepped forward, raised her cane, and bopped Michael right on the top of his head. Real hard. "That's enough," she said. "Michael, don't you hurt my baby."

Michael grabbed his cap off the floor and we went up to his room to smoke some pot. He told me, "She's my sister and I love her, but, Kevin, that bitch is crazy!"

The HBO special was a huge success. Whitney received better press than she had had in a long time and record sales were brisk, especially her single of the national anthem. Her 1991 concert tour for *I'm Your Baby Tonight* was set to go in April with Lexington, Kentucky, one of the first stops. She was traveling with her usual entourage of about twenty, including, of course, Robyn Crawford. Michael went along as his sister's bodyguard, and there was also another bodyguard, Dave Roberts. After checking into their hotel they decided to go to the harness races before dinner. When they returned to the hotel, all hell broke loose.

I was in my beauty salon the next day when the morning paper arrived and I couldn't believe what I saw. An article said something like, "Superstar Whitney Houston in slugfest in Lexington, Kentucky!" Reportedly, Whitney, her bodyguard brother Michael, and several other members of her group had been in a fistfight with fans at the Radisson Plaza Hotel. I rushed over to Regina's to find out what she knew about it, and she filled me in. She had already spoken with Whitney that morning but was standing by for more news.

Regina said they had gone to Red Mile Harness Racetrack and were having a good time betting and drinking. However, when they started losing money, their mood changed. Michael can get a little surly when he's drinking, and that he had lost money at the track only made him feel worse. When they got back to the hotel, the drinking continued and so did everyone's bad mood. The Evander Holyfield–George Foreman match was being televised that night, so everyone decided they would watch it in the hotel lounge and try to forget their bad luck at the track. They just wanted to be left alone, but that was impossible as soon as the crowd saw Whitney. They surged around her, asking for autographs and gushing over her, making it impossible for her to view the boxing match.

Her bodyguard, Dave Roberts, who is British, politely asked everyone to leave, explaining that Ms. Houston wanted to relax and watch the fight; they could get her autograph the next evening after her concert. Apparently they were die-hard fans or just rude, because they refused to leave and kept pestering her. Finally Dave Roberts stood up and said loudly, "Piss off, all of you! Ms. Houston doesn't wish to be bothered just now."

The autograph seekers left but were soon replaced by another group of fans, and again Dave yelled, "Piss off!" Onlookers say that Whitney's mood was becoming more arrogant and so was Michael's.

It was pretty rowdy that night with more men than women in the lounge, and they were all ogling the beautiful singing star, trying to catch her eye. Three men were sitting at a nearby table and talking real loud, laughing, poking each other, watching Whitney. Booze was flowing and the men took offense at being told to "piss off" by some pansy Englishman, so they muttered a couple of insults and Michael and Dave answered in kind. The men then made some racial slurs and a few sexually explicit remarks. Whitney had had enough. She had tried to ignore them and watch the fight, but they wouldn't leave her alone. She said, "Come on, let's get out of here. We can watch the fight in our rooms."

Everyone went their separate ways, and Whitney, Michael, and Robyn took the elevator up to their rooms. When they got off at their floor, the same three men were waiting for them, insisting that Whitney give them her autograph. Michael told them to "back off," but the guys were drunk and belligerent, and one of them threw a punch at Michael. He punched back, knocking the man on his ass. The guy's buddies jumped into the melee and racist slurs began flying. One of them called Whitney a "stuck-up nigger bitch," and that's when Michael lost it. He wasn't about to let a bunch of redneck yahoos insult his baby sister.

Fists were flying. It was three against one, and even though Michael was holding his own, Whitney flipped. She jumped on the back of one of the men and began slugging him, then delivered a solid blow to the jaw of one of the other men, knocking him off Michael. Everybody was screaming and cussing, punching, and rolling around on the floor. Doors were being flung open up and down the long corridor. Guests of the ritzy, luxurious Radisson Plaza Hotel couldn't believe their eyes. The elegant and beautiful superstar Whitney Houston, cussing like a sailor and delivering punches that would have made George Foreman proud! One of the guests said they heard her yell, "You're going to die, you son of a bitch!"

Someone had called the police and they broke it up and calmed the combatants down. But it wasn't over yet. The trio of men filed a lawsuit against Whitney and Michael, charging them both with assault.

I was at Regina's when Whitney called and told her about the confrontation. She was laughing and said she'd kicked ass, baby. She wasn't about to let those "hillbilly motherfuckers" hurt her brother. Michael was injured pretty badly. Besides the expected cuts, scrapes, and bruises, he had a concussion and some cracked knuckles. It's a miracle Whitney wasn't hurt in the free-for-all, but she walked away unscathed. The only thing worrying her was the threatened lawsuit, and she asked Regina how to handle it. Regina didn't think it was anything to be concerned about, but I did. I told Whitney if the men sued her, to sue them back. "On what charges?" she asked.

"Invasion of privacy," I said, "as well as assault and battery and defamation of character. After all, it was your name that was splashed all over the newspapers."

Just a few days later, Whitney and Michael were served with a summons to appear in court, and Whitney countersued. But she took it a step further, making a public statement that the three men had tried to blackmail her, demanding $425,000 from her or they would sell their story to the press. This wasn't true. She had concocted the story to make herself look better, but then, Whitney always was a little dramatic.

The press had a field day. Hardly a day went by without some account appearing in some newspaper about the battling Houstons and how the diva of pop had reverted to her hardscrabble youth, taking on thugs who were beating up her brother. It got so bad, John Houston called a press conference and told reporters that he was "very proud that Michael maintained his dignity and professionalism by not responding to the verbal abuse directed toward Whitney."

He continued, "In the face of this restraint, these men shrewdly concluded that the only way they could achieve a situation that would create the sensationalized media attention they desired was to attack Michael physically without cause or provocation. I'm equally proud of my daughter, Whitney, who would not let any career concerns prevent her from protecting her brother. By exposing herself to potential physical harm, she risked career-threatening injuries."

Whitney told Regina she was so proud of her father for publicly supporting her. They had been estranged ever since he ran off with her maid, but this seemed to bring them back together. Whitney was devastated that the press continued to hound her, to poke microphones in her face and ask about the fight in Kentucky. "How could this have happened?" she said to me over the phone one day. "This is so bad. How could Michael and I have gotten involved like this?"

I told her that we all knew Michael had a temper, especially when he was drinking, and for Whitney and her brother to go into what was basically a "white" bar was courting trouble. I figured there probably weren't a whole lot of blacks there that night, not in Lexington, Kentucky.

"We tried to ignore them," Whitney said. "We just wanted to have a couple of drinks and watch the fight, but they wouldn't leave us alone."

Fayette County attorney Norrie Wake researched the incident and interviewed witnesses on both sides of the fracas, finally determining that Whitney's camp was the most believable. He stated that they had been unduly provoked and that "contradictory evidence would have made conviction impossible."

That the three men had gone directly to the press with their story proved that they were out for whatever notoriety they could garner from this unfortunate incident.

"I wish you'd been there, Kevin," Whitney told me. "The motherfuckers would've *died!*"

When the tour was in Miami, Whitney asked Regina to see if I would join them as her bodyguard. Michael was traveling with her and so was her older half brother, Gary, but for some reason she wanted me along as well. I was thrilled and quickly agreed. When I arrived in Florida, Whitney gave me my own I'M YOUR BABY TONIGHT jumpsuit, which everyone who worked for her wore, as well as a custom-made satin jacket with my name embroidered on it.

As excited as I was about traveling with Whitney Houston and experiencing all the perks of being with a superstar, I soon realized this was the tour from hell. I saw firsthand what was going on behind the scenes, and it wasn't a pretty picture. There was so much stress and strife all the time I didn't see how Whitney could put on a decent show.

Everybody was doing drugs and drinking and hopping from bed to bed. Bobby Brown was calling Whitney all the time, and this made Robyn so jealous she would sleep with the dancers in the group and several times even with Michael just to annoy

Whitney. Whatever dancers that were left over were passed between Michael and Gary. The threat of violence always lurked just below the surface. It was total chaos.

The concert tour was in serious trouble due to the bad press and Whitney's attitude, but it limped along with Whitney giving only lackadaisical performances. She was always late, sometimes up to two hours, and would be met by an angry, booing crowd. To add insult to injury, she didn't bother to apologize or even make up some excuse for her tardiness; she just didn't give a damn. She still had a lot of loyal fans, however, and when they tried to approach her for autographs, she would freeze them in their tracks with the coldest, most withering look imaginable. Some of her fans grumbled to the press that "Whitney Houston is a real bitch in person. She treats her fans like garbage. I'll never buy another video of hers again."

In August 1991, my family finally got a chance to meet Whitney when she did a show at the World Music Center in Tinley Park, Illinois. She had arranged for my mother, brothers, and sisters to have front row center seats, and I was proud to be a part of her entourage. She was sweet to my mother and made a big fuss over her. Mom was thrilled to meet such a big star and I was grateful to Whitney for being so kind.

Nineteen ninety-one was the most horrible year of Whitney's life, both personally and professionally. As Queen Elizabeth once said of her royal family, "It was an *annus horribilis*" (a horrible year). Whitney had started calling her people at Nippy, Inc. "the Royal Family," so when she heard Queen Elizabeth's remark on TV, she agreed 100 percent. She said to me once, "There's so fucking much backstabbing and lying and jealousy and intrigue going on around me, I feel like one of the Windsors!"

She was stressed-out and no doubt was worrying about the drop in ticket sales to her concerts. A couple of concerts were actually canceled due to lack of interest, but the Royal Family limped on anyway.

Whitney's voice was not what it had once been. She was hoarse and a little gravelly and couldn't reach those high, clear notes that had once been her trademark. The press reported that she was suffering from a "throat condition," but I knew the real reason. She was sucking up that weed more and more as her life seemed to crumble around her. Regina said Whitney had always indulged in pot to relax, so did everyone in the Royal Family. But this past year she'd started sprinkling a little cocaine in with the marijuana before she rolled a joint.

On tour I got to know Robyn pretty well, and to my surprise, I liked her. I had heard so many negative things about her from Regina and Cissy, I was expecting a real dragon lady, but she was okay. She dressed like a man everywhere she went. If she wasn't wearing a men's business suit, she would appear in jeans and a men's shirt. And she also wore men's shoes. She was madly in love with Whitney and didn't care who knew it. She told me she had been looking out for Whitney ever since they were teenagers when the other kids had picked on them and called them dykes and she had had to "kick some ass." She was strong-willed and domineering by nature, so it just seemed normal for her to protect the person she loved.

From Florida we traveled to Virginia, New York, Philadelphia, New Jersey, Detroit, and Los Angeles. By this time I felt like a seasoned old pro and had learned more about Whitney Houston than I ever really wanted to know. This complex lady had many sides, and I was being introduced to them all on a daily basis.

In late October 1991, the Thirteenth Annual Black Achievement Awards was being held in Los Angeles, and I would be going as Whitney's guest. We checked into the Westwood Marquis, and Whitney called, telling Regina to phone Bobby Brown to let him know she had to go to rehearsal and that she would meet him later. After a little nap and a shower, I went to the theater to watch the rehearsal. All these big stars I'd heard about or admired were there: Patti LaBelle, Dionne Warwick, Gladys Knight, Della Reese, Mario Van Peebles, Jasmine Guy, and Wesley Snipes, among others.

Just as we were leaving our hotel room on the way to the show that night, Regina said, "Kevin, please don't try to socialize with any the stars, okay? Security will see that you're nobody and throw you out." I was shocked and hurt, but I kept my mouth shut, refusing to let her ruin this magical night for me.

John Houston was waiting outside, alone, and he asked us if we would ride with him to the theater. As we entered a beautiful black Lincoln Town Car, Regina whispered, "I wonder if Nippy knows she paid for Daddy's car tonight?"

I sat with John as Regina kissed me and said, "I have to go do my job. See you backstage after the show."

Mario Van Peebles introduced Patti LaBelle, and when she walked onstage, she looked directly at me and gave me a big smile. She sang her new release, "Somebody Loves You, Baby," and all during the number she kept making eye contact with me. Then she did the unthinkable: she reached down and motioned for me to join her onstage. "Come on, baby," she said. "Come on and dance with me." We danced together and the crowd was screaming and applauding and Patti said, "Sing with me, honey," and I did.

What a rush I got. I sat down in my seat to watch the rest of the show, but I couldn't concentrate. All I could think about were those few magical moments onstage.

As described earlier, I went backstage where Patti complimented me on my voice and asked if I had management. If not, she said, she would be interested in handling my career. I said, no, I didn't, but out of nowhere, Whitney came rushing over and said, "Yes, he does. I'm going to manage his career."

Patti and I spoke for a few more minutes, and she asked if she'd see me at the After Party and I said, "Sure, I'll be there," but Whitney had another idea.

"I want you and Regina to come to my house for a little get-together," she said. "I want you to meet Bobby."

I would much rather have gone to the party, but I knew I shouldn't say anything. When Whitney gave a summons, you had better show up!

Only the five of us were there: Robyn, Whitney, Bobby, me, and Regina. Whitney changed into a pair of silk pj's and we just relaxed, drank beer, smoked weed, and gossiped about the show. Bobby was also different from what I had heard about him. He was down-to-earth and intelligent and mature for his age. I liked him a lot, but it was clear who did not like him. Robyn just sat there all night, glaring at him.

The Royal Family were on their way to London next. I had never been out of the States before so I was excited. However, I didn't travel with Whitney. I joined the tour later. I had been gone a long time and wanted to see my wife and sons before venturing overseas. In England, I caught a taxi at Heathrow Airport and headed to Chelsea Harbor, stopping along the way to buy roses for Regina and Whitney.

Regina met me at the hotel and we just had time for some quick lovemaking before meeting the others. Whitney was scheduled to speak at Piccadilly Park to a group of children with AIDS. The regulars were all there with Whitney when Regina and I got off the elevator: Michael and his girlfriend, Robyn, Dave Roberts, Sylvia, and Smitty, the driver. We piled into a big van and took off, everyone laughing, joking, and having a good time. I'd missed being with them. Whitney was talking to me and Robyn kept interrupting until finally Whitney turned on her and snapped, "Shut the fuck up before I kick your ass out!"

I chuckled, thinking she was kidding, but she was serious. "I mean it, Kevin," she said. "I'll beat this bitch's ass and put her out alongside the road. Just ask her what happened yesterday on the paddleboats."

"Huh," Robyn snorted. "Nothing happened on the paddleboats and you fucking well know it."

"You fucking liar," Whitney yelled. "You know damn well I beat your ass and made you walk back to the hotel!"

Robyn glared and muttered, "We beat each other's ass, okay?"

I still wasn't used to Whitney's language. She cussed like

some kind of low-life ghetto broad. I don't think she was capable of speaking a sentence without using the word *fuck* someplace. Then in public, she slipped on the ladylike demeanor as easily as pulling a dress over her head, suddenly becoming the proper young lady who had been raised in church. It was quite a contrast.

We were met at the park by several policemen, who directed us to the stage, and Whitney grabbed my hand, telling me to stay close to her. Children were everywhere, yelling, "Whitney! Whitney! Whitney!"

She ran onstage, with me close behind, and began her speech, telling the kids how much she loved them and how they were all in her prayers every night. She said that God's love and strength would see them through these troubling times, and to always remember that God loved them and was watching over them. She then jumped off the stage and held out her arms and the kids flocked forward, engulfing her. She was crying and hugging them and kissing them as they chanted her name, and I was really moved. I thought, *Wow, she really does love these little kids!* A dozen photographers swarmed around, snapping pictures of Whitney's lovely, tearstained face.

She then turned and motioned to me and I took her hand and helped her back onstage. She was still smiling and waving, but under her breath she said to me, "Get me the fuck out of here, away from these musty-assed, smelly kids!" I stared at her and she was dry eyed; the tears had completely vanished.

Later over dinner we were talking and she told me I reminded her of Bobby Brown in many ways. "You're both good people," she said. "I can see the gold in your eyes. You're real." She asked me what my sign was, and when I told her Aquarius, she said, "So is Bobby. When's your birthday?"

"February fifth."

"You've got to be kidding. That's Bobby's birthday, too. No wonder you remind me so much of him." She said she was a Leo and Aquarius was her love sign.

The next evening while Whitney was performing, I asked

Robyn what she thought of Bobby Brown, and she snorted and said he was a punk—not good enough to wipe Whitney's feet. "She'll never go out with him. She's got better taste than that!"

I wasn't too sure about that. I had seen a certain look in Whitney's eyes when she talked about him, and I had a feeling she would be calling him when we returned to the States. Then all hell would break loose.

Robyn what she thought of Bobby Brown, and she snorted and said he was a punk—not good enough to wipe Whitney's feet. "She'll never go out with him. She's got better taste than that!"

I wasn't too sure about that. I had seen a certain look in Whitney's eyes when she talked about him, and I had a feeling she would be calling him when we returned to the States. Then all hell would break loose.

8

Who Is the *Real* Bobby Brown?

THE YEAR 1991 ENDED NOT WITH A CELEBRATION BUT A SHOCKER when John Houston married Peggy Griffith on December 28. The wedding was held in John's condo in Fort Lee, New Jersey, presided over by Rev. Harry Spellman of the Macedonia Church of Christ. There were fewer than a dozen guests and not one member of John's immediate family, not his sons and most certainly not Whitney. By mutual agreement, everyone boycotted the nuptials. When the press tried to reach Whitney for a comment, they were met with a cold, stony silence from the Royal Family.

In one of the rare moments when Robyn was actually being civil to Regina, she told her that John had only married Peggy because he had learned that Cissy was having an affair with the pastor of their church and he wanted to hurt and embarrass her as badly as she had embarrassed him. Even though they had been separated for many years, John still felt a certain "ownership" as far as Cissy was concerned, and the affair infuriated and humiliated him. He still wanted the media to think the Houstons were a God-fearing, tight-knit, loving Christian family who worshiped and clung together in times of need.

Many times at different public functions and business meetings, I'd watched John swagger about, pushing people around, snapping out orders like a drill sergeant, making sure that everybody knew *he* was in charge of Nippy, Inc., and therefore in charge of Whitney. I once told Regina, "You know, John would make one hell of a good dictator for some little third world country!"

But for all his pomposity and bombastic rantings, he felt demeaned that he was working for his daughter, that without her he would be back in Newark working at a menial job. He was earning $125,000 a year as her "manager," but that was a mere pittance compared to Whitney's earnings. "It's just chump change," a member of the Royal Family told me. "She's throwing him a bone so he won't feel like such a failure."

After John married Whitney's ex-maid, she went into a deep depression and stayed secluded in her house not talking to anyone except Robyn, Regina, and a few close friends.

Whitney felt betrayed by both her parents. The '91 tour had proved a bitter disappointment, the first time a Whitney Houston tour had not been a success. For it to end this way was almost more than Whitney could bear. The holidays were pretty grim for the Royal Family in 1991 and Whitney was dreading what 1992 would bring.

As I had predicted in London, as soon as Whitney returned, she got in touch with Bobby. If ever anyone needed a little TLC, it was Whitney, and obviously bad boy Bobby Brown knew just how to apply it. He was living in Atlanta with his son, Landon, and his father, Herbert.

After their affair became public, Whitney told a reporter she'd been attracted to Bobby right from the start because he was so different and because he *didn't* put her on a pedestal like most

(Above) Whitney and her
parents, John Houston
and Cissy Houston
(Corkery/Globe)

(Right) Cissy and daugh-
ter Whitney in a proud
moment in 1980
(Czvekus/Retna)

(Left) Whitney Houston, Kevin Ammons, and Robyn Crawford (personal collection of Kevin Ammons)

(Below) A happy family: Whitney, Bobby, and their adorable daughter Bobbi. (Green/Globe)

(Above) Whitney and Clive Davis, music impresario, in 1990 (McGee/Globe)

(Left) Jermaine Jackson, who sang a duet with Whitney on the soap opera As The World Turns *(Rodriguez/Globe)*

*(Opposite) Whitney at the
1986 Grammys
(Grossman/Globe)*

*(Above) Robyn Crawford,
Whitney's "close personal
friend" (Barrett/Globe)*

*(Right) Robyn Crawford
at the Tampa Airport in
Florida (Barrett/Globe)*

(Above) Whitney and her brother, Michael (Globe/Barrett)

(Left) Michael Houston (Whitney's brother) and Kevin Ammons (personal collection of Kevin Ammons)

(Opposite) Whitney Houston and Bobby Brown at a gala for the T. J. Martel Foundation in 1995 (Hartman/Globe)

The Ammons Brothers: Craig, Lee, Kevin (rear), Darrell Nelson (front) (Bob Dooley/personal collection of Kevin Ammons)

men. "Before I met Bobby, I always got that 'How can I show you I'm worthy?' attitude from guys, but with Bobby it was simple. He knew what I needed was love."

Whitney would take off for Atlanta to see Bobby, but she would phone Regina first and tell her if Robyn called, to tell her, "You don't know where I am." And Robyn would call. And call. She demanded to know where Whitney was, but Regina wouldn't tell her. "If she had wanted you to know where she was, she would have told you."

I could hear Robyn cussing and yelling over the phone: "You fucking liar. I'm going to kick your ass!"

"Fuck you, you fucking dyke," Regina would say. "I'm not worried about you." She would hang up, and seconds later Robyn would call back, but Regina wouldn't answer. She'd let the answering machine pick up. Robyn would scream obscenities, threatening Regina with physical harm and even death unless she picked up the phone and told her where Whitney was. Regina would just laugh. She loved to torment Robyn and now she could do it with Whitney's blessing. The calls would continue all night long, but we'd turn off the sound so we wouldn't be bothered.

One day I was at Regina's alone when Robyn called, and she sounded so miserable, my heart went out to her. When she realized I wasn't going to hang up the phone, she started crying and told me her heart was breaking. She said she knew Whitney was with some guy, and she suspected it was that punk gangster Bobby Brown.

She said, "I'm the only person in Whitney's life who has given her unconditional love; everybody else just uses her, even her parents. *Most especially* her parents. Both of them are riding her coattails. If it wasn't for Whitney, they'd be on welfare. I don't understand why she supports them. They've never supported her—financially, I mean. It was only after Whitney started getting famous that they began showing all their so-called support and praising God for their talented little Nippy. When Whitney and I first got together, it was a different story. We were living in a crummy little one-room apartment with no refrigerator and very little food, but nobody helped us. Nobody offered a helping hand. The only helping hand that's ever been offered to Whitney is mine."

She went on to say that all the Houstons hated her and wanted her dead; they blamed her because Whitney was gay. "But she's more bi than gay," Robyn said. "She likes guys, too, and it tears me up."

Robyn had good reason to be worried. The friendship between Whitney and Bobby was swiftly blossoming into something much deeper. She spent every spare moment with Bobby and talked openly to the press about him. And this was something she'd *never* done in the past, feeling the way she did about the media. But suddenly photographs started appearing in newspapers with a beaming Whitney clinging to Bobby's arm and practically cooing, "He's a cool, down-to-earth, sexy man."

When I was at Regina's, I noticed she would sometimes take the phone into the bathroom to talk, and when I asked her about it, she would say, "It's nothing," but I'm a curious guy, so one day I stood at the door and listened. She was talking to an editor of one of the tabloids, selling them information about Whitney and Bobby!

This shocked me and I started to listen at other times when she had the phone in the bathroom. On several occasions she told stories about Michael Jackson, too. I knew she was close friends with Michael's publicist, Bob Jones, and on many occasions Jones would call her and tell her about the latest fiasco in his client's life. Regina would then call the tabloids and relate the story, changing it just enough so Jones wouldn't know where the item came from.

I finally confronted her because I felt what she was doing was wrong. She was not only betraying her boss, Whitney, but her friendship with Jones as well. She simply shrugged and told me to "grow up. Lots of stars plant stories about themselves in the rags. Let's face it, where else can they get ten million readers per week. That's a lot of publicity, baby."

Because of her friendship with Bob Jones, I learned about the allegations against Michael Jackson long before they became public. Rumors had been floating around for years about Michael's sexual preference, or if he even had any, and it was well-known in the industry that he was gay. It was also well-known that he cared deeply for children and had donated millions of dollars to different charities in their behalf. But to discover that his sexual preference *was* children came as a real shock to many people.

"This is gonna destroy his career," Regina said.

For the first time in many months, Whitney was happy and eagerly looking forward to her future. She decided it was time to make a firm commitment to Kevin Costner abut doing the movie with him. Her disastrous 1991 concert tour had left a deep scar, and she wanted to distance herself from music for a while. Her affair with Bobby was her most fulfilling experience and she told everyone she wanted to marry him and have "lots and lots of babies."

The media went into a feeding frenzy, scrambling about trying to dig up any information they could about the new man in Whitney's life. Just who was this young, hip-hop bad boy who had done what no other man had been able to do—steal the heart of America's Sweetheart? He was born Bobby Baresford Brown in 1969, which made him six years younger than Whitney, just twenty-three years old to her twenty-nine. It was a big age difference and some tabloids accused her of getting a boy young enough so she could raise him her way.

"Bobby was never a kid," said producer Teddy Riley. "He was born and raised in the 'hood. He was runnin' with gangs by the time he was ten years old, and by the time he was twelve, he'd been stabbed and shot and seen a lot of his homeboys killed in the street."

Bobby's mother, Carole, told reporters the only thing that kept her son alive was his dream of someday becoming a singing star. By the mideighties, when he was about fourteen years old, he joined a group called New Edition, a hard-edge rapping version of the old Jackson Five. They were pretty successful for such a young bunch of guys, especially with teenage girls, but Bobby wanted more. He didn't want to be "just one of the guys." He wanted a solo career, so in 1986 he left New Edition and went out on his own. It was a good move. His first record, "My Prerogative," hit number one. He had just turned seventeen.

His first album didn't do all that well, but his second, *Don't Be Cruel,* sold 8 million copies in 1988. During his concert tour he tore up the stage with his sexy gyrations and lewd hand movements (simulating masturbation), earning him the title of "R&B's raunchy bad boy," which was soon shortened to just "Bad Boy."

In 1989's world tour he was arrested in Georgia for "lewd and licentious behavior," and it shocked some sense into him. He decided he had better get his priorities straight if he wanted to be a big star. When he met Whitney later that year at the Soul Train Music Awards, he realized that the beautiful pop diva was his number one priority and he set out to win her. It wouldn't be easy, not with Robyn and Cissy both against the relationship. Cissy thought he was "just a little boy" and an unsuitable one at that. He had two children out of wedlock and showed no sign of settling down. He was "ugly and vulgar" onstage, thumbing his nose at convention, and Cissy seriously doubted if he had ever set foot inside a church.

She tried to caution Whitney about Bobby, but her daughter wasn't listening to anything her mother had to say, not about her career and not about her love life. While most kids rebel during their teenage years, Whitney was now rebelling in her late twenties. She'd been under her mother's control for too long, and she wasn't going to stay there any longer. She found Cissy's interference in her life intrusive and annoying, and she shut her out completely. She was a grown woman almost thirty years old, earning a staggering amount of money, and known the world over. So who was Cissy to tell her what to do?

Robyn had usurped Cissy's power a long time ago, leaving the older woman feeling unwanted and unimportant. She complained to friends that she couldn't get close to her own daughter without an appointment and that "a mother's opinion doesn't matter anymore." But that didn't stop her from voicing her views to anyone else who would listen. She hated that in Whitney's first big starring role in a motion picture she would have an interracial love affair. She told friends she didn't want to see her daughter become intimate with a white man, adding, "We've all worked too hard to take a chance like this." As usual, she was trying to put herself in her daughter's shoes, as if it were *her* movie, *her* first starring role, *she'd* been the one who had worked so hard for this chance. The sad truth was, she just couldn't let go. This was the closest she had ever come to fame, and now she was being nudged out of even the limelight's distant glow.

In February 1992, Whitney flew to Miami to begin shooting *The Bodyguard,* but before she left, she told her parents she was pregnant and Bobby Brown was the father. Regina told me that Cissy "came unglued. She was furious and began ranting and raving about what a punk Bobby was and how this relationship would never work—it was the biggest mistake of Whitney's life." But Whitney told Cissy she was in love, she was having this baby, and that was pretty much that!

Kevin Costner was producing the movie himself and had done his homework well. As was his habit with any movie role he undertook, he had researched meticulously, learning all he could about a bodyguard's dangerous occupation. He had hired bodyguards for himself in the past and understood the relationship between guard and celebrity. Like other major stars, Costner had had his share of overly zealous fans and had felt the fear that comes from being surrounded by thousands of screaming, hysterical strangers all wanting a piece of him.

"There's always an element of fear when a celebrity goes out in public," he said. "We all remember John Lennon, Rebecca Shafer, the Kennedys, Presidents Ford and Reagan, and so many others who were shot or killed by deranged lunatics. It's scary, but knowing we have a bodyguard helps."

Whitney agreed. Several bodyguards had always traveled with her, and she had beefed up her security even more after the fiasco in Kentucky. Both she and Costner went into this film with a personal knowledge of stars and bodyguards, and it would serve them well during shooting.

In late March, less than a month into filming, Whitney suffered a miscarriage. Bobby was recording in Atlanta when she called him, and he rushed to Miami. "That's when the Royal Family started believing that just maybe this guy was really serious about Whitney and she about him," Regina said. "Up until then, we all thought, 'Oh, he's just another boy toy. She'll get bored and everything will go back to normal.' "

That wasn't the case, however. The tragedy brought them even closer together. Whitney was heartbroken. She wanted babies, and most importantly she wanted Bobby's babies. Depressed and sad, she often called Regina, crying over the phone. It couldn't have been more than a couple of days after her miscarriage when the *National Enquirer* hit the stands with this headline: "Pregnant Whitney Houston Loses Her Love Child!"

Whitney called Regina in a rage, demanding to know who at Nippy, Inc. had betrayed her. She knew it had to be an inside leak because only a handful of people knew. Regina promised to look into it, but I suspected it was Regina herself. She had been leaking items to the rags for years, and to cover herself she always had the check made out to one of her relatives or friends so it couldn't be traced back to her.

Legitimate newspapers began calling Whitney and asking her to either confirm or deny the *Enquirer* article, but she told them she didn't want to discuss her private life, hoping they would leave her alone at such a tragic time. She should have known better. Her silence only whetted their appetite, so she reluctantly spoke with a reporter from *USA Today,* hoping it would get all the rest of the reporters off her back.

"Let's say I did have a miscarriage. That's *my* business. You know what I'm saying? It just so happens it happened while I was doing a movie, on a movie set. People get word and people call up the papers and tell them. Miscarriages happen to women all the time. It's just that I'm this—this *person,* Whitney Houston."

Filming continued on *The Bodyguard* and Whitney threw herself completely into the work, hoping to take her mind off the loss of her baby. Bobby called every day and flew into town when his schedule permitted. They went out to dinner one evening, and on the way home, Bobby proposed. He held out a ring box with a small, modest diamond and somehow managed to keep a straight face until she said yes. Then, giggling like a kid, he tossed it away and whipped out a magnificent ten-carat diamond that took her breath away.

"He is just so cute," Whitney told Jamie Foster Brown, publisher of *Sister 2 Sister.* "He played me like I was Atari."

"I just wanted to see if she'd marry me even if I had nothin'," he said, grinning.

"They're just kids," Jamie Brown would say later, commenting on Whitney's reference to the game Atari. "In the scheme of things they've never been allowed to develop in terms of character growth that a normal person would have."

When I heard about the engagement, I knew the shit was going to hit the fan, and it did. I was in Los Angeles with Regina, and as we were lying in bed one morning, pretty early, we heard this loud knocking on the door downstairs. I answered it and Robyn was standing there, looking like death. Her face was haggard and her eyes were swollen and hollow-looking. I told her Regina and I were still in bed but to come on upstairs if she wanted to talk.

She started crying then, just great big, gulping, hysterical sobs that shook her whole body. She bent over, gripping her stomach as if she were in real physical pain as she stumbled upstairs with me. I was concerned and thought she was having an appendicitis attack or something and asked if she wanted me to call a doctor.

"No," she mumbled, and her voice was real low, like a dying

person struggling to speak. "I won't let her do it. She can't marry Bobby. I won't let her do it."

She was still doubled over, clutching her stomach, and tears were soaking her face. I put my arm around her shoulders and gently led her to the bed and told her to rest for a minute. She lay down on her side, drawing her knees up tight against her chest and wrapping her arms around them. She was moaning and shaking, her shoulders just heaving with pain. She kept mumbling over and over, "She can't do it—I won't let her do it, she just can't marry him."

I was really uncomfortable and completely out of my element. I didn't know what to do so I went downstairs to see about getting some coffee. I felt I should leave the two women together so I busied myself while they stayed upstairs. About half an hour later, they came downstairs and Robyn had pulled herself together. In fact, she looked pretty much like the old Robyn I was used to seeing and told me thanks and left.

I looked at Regina and she shook her head and said, "She's in a bad way, baby. She said if Whitney went through with this marriage, she'd kill herself."

When I returned to Chicago, Whitney called me and told me she hadn't forgotten her promise to manage my singing career. She said she had been blown away by my voice when I sang with Patti LaBelle and she thought I had what it took to be a big star. She was busy shooting *The Bodyguard* but told me to call her father and set up some studio time to record a demo. She said she would pay for everything.

I didn't waste time getting my band together. We went into the studio and recorded three songs, but I could never reach John about payment for the studio time. About three weeks passed and I just said, "Fuck it," and paid the $2,800 bill myself. I was anxiously waiting for Whitney to complete the movie so she could listen to my demos, but that would be several months away. I kept myself busy with my beauty salon and other business interests, but one eye was always on the calendar.

When Kevin Costner first approached Whitney about doing the movie with him, he had promised her that he would protect her and make sure she wasn't called on to do anything she didn't feel comfortable with. After she read the script, she met with Costner and told him she thought Rachel, the character she was playing, was *too* hard and bitchy.

"People will think it's typecasting for sure," she said, laughing. "Everybody's always saying what a bitch I am. I'd feel better if Rachel was a little nicer, a little softer. I mean, sure, we all have our bitchy days, but in the script she goes around pissed off all the time."

Costner agreed and the part was rewritten to Whitney's satisfaction. I give her a lot of credit for taking on a project as demanding as *The Bodyguard* when she had had absolutely no experience as an actress. Critics had their say about it, of course, speculating whether the diva of pop could make the transition into movie star, and *Rolling Stone* magazine cornered her for an interview.

"I was concerned that people would dog me before they gave me an opportunity to do the job," she said. "I wanted to do some acting, but I mean, I never thought I'd be costarring with Kevin Costner! I thought 'I'll just get this *little* part somewhere and I'll work my way up.' And all of sudden I get this script, and I said, 'I don't know. This is kind of —big.' I was scared."

Director Mick Jackson said, "It was either teach an actress to sing or, as with Whitney, teach a singer to act. Her life as a pop diva means that everything is set to her requirements, which is totally different from shooting a film. When she got a look at the shooting schedule, the first thing she said was, 'I'm *not* a day person.' "

But she *was* a trouper, and she threw herself into the role with determination and concentration. She wanted to make this work. She needed a success after all the disasters that had befallen her in the past year. Everybody was saying that her biggest problem would be Bobby Brown. Rumors were circulating that he was jealous of Kevin Costner and afraid that Whitney would take her role "too seriously" and fall in love with the handsome movie star.

"That's bullshit," Whitney scoffed. "I didn't go into this movie wanting to fall in love with Kevin Costner. I was already in love with Bobby. Being that he's my man, I talked to him about the movie and let him read the script. At some moments along the way, he did say, 'Well, how are these scenes going to be played? How much are you going to be involved with this?' and so on. But Bobby knew me and trusted me. I was not in the movie to be with a sex symbol. It wasn't about sex. Bobby was comfortable with that. You have to have a trust between the two of you. I think Bobby and I have that."

9

Whitney, Robyn, and the Bad Boy of R&B

WHEN CISSY LEARNED ABOUT WHITNEY'S ENGAGEMENT TO BOBBY, she took out her Christian cloak, which was always close at hand, and sniffed that Bobby wasn't good enough for her baby. "We're a strict Christian family," she said. "We have morals and we believe in God and family. Bobby Brown obviously does not. He already has two children born out of wedlock—that we know about—and he had no qualms about getting our daughter pregnant before any vows were spoken. This is not the kind of young man I want as a son-in-law!"

Robyn put it more succinctly: "He's a punk. I don't like him."

Even John Houston, who usually didn't become involved in personal problems, met with Whitney and asked her to reconsider, to think carefully before marrying. "If you don't," he said gravely, "you'll be making the biggest mistake of your life. And you'll break your mother's heart."

Whitney didn't listen to anybody. She was happy. So what if Bobby had "a past. We've all got a past." Soon that past would become the present and cause her to wonder if, indeed, she was doing the right thing. One of the tabloids printed a story that bad boy Bobby had just become a father—for the third time. And the mother was most certainly *not* his fiancée. The mother of Bobby's new son was a woman he'd grown up with in the Orchard Park projects and she was also the mother of his two-year-old daughter.

Whitney was furious and told Regina she felt humiliated and embarrassed. How could Bobby want anything to do with another woman when he had *her*? He had a lot of explaining to do, and apparently he did it very well. He convinced Whitney that the woman was definitely in his past, telling her that once he had become involved with her, Whitney, he had broken off all past relationships. Unfortunately, he didn't know the woman was already pregnant at the time. He swore he had been faithful ever since he and Whitney started dating. She believed him and the engagement ring stayed on her finger.

I found out later that Robyn had hired a private investigator to check out Bobby's past to see if she could dig up any dirt on him. When she found out about the woman he had had a romance with since they were teenagers, she also discovered the woman had recently given birth to the second of Bobby's babies. She was counting on Whitney's famous temper to break off the engagement. But her plot backfired.

During the shooting of *The Bodyguard* Whitney took some time out to repair her image and promote the movie. ABC-TV aired a special, "Whitney Houston: This Is My Life," giving the public a glimpse into a superstar's daily activities. She was filmed at Nippy, Inc., as a corporate head interacting with her staff, then visiting with both of her parents, relaxing at home in her lavish mansion, and emoting with Kevin Costner on the set of *The Bodyguard*.

Production was now winding down, and as Costner and director Mick Jackson viewed the footage, they realized they had a problem. For all Whitney's beauty and sexuality, she came across stiff and cold on film. The love that was supposed to be developing between her character and Costner's just wasn't there.

"There was no chemistry," Jackson said. "They looked like a couple of pals passing the time of day instead of the torrid lovers they were supposed to be."

Costner had a clause in his contract giving him the option of reediting the final cut of the film if he wasn't happy with the director's cut. He wasn't happy. He had promised Whitney that if she did this movie with him, he would "make her look good," and she didn't look as good as he thought she could. He knew this was her first role, that she was a singer, not an actress, and he felt it was his responsibility to do right by her. Her classic beauty shone through in every scene, however, so he cut some of the more difficult speaking parts and concentrated on her face and body.

In the final cut, there are lots of close-ups of her large, almond-shaped eyes, wistful and a little sad, reflecting her fear and uncertainty. The camera lingers on her sensual body and graceful movements. The heart-tugging strains of the theme song, "I Will Always Love You," play in the background, providing poignancy where none had existed.

"I Will Always Love You" had been written by country singer Dolly Parton over two decades earlier, and she had enjoyed a small success with it. When Whitney recorded it, it zoomed up the charts to number one, becoming a megahit.

With filming completed on the movie, Whitney turned her attention to planning her wedding. At first, she and Bobby had wanted simply to elope and avoid the press they knew would hound them, but Cissy wouldn't hear of it. If her stubborn daughter insisted on going through with this marriage, then Cissy wanted it to be a wedding to remember. She did not have a big fancy wedding herself, so once again she was living her life vicariously through Whitney.

With Cissy's reluctant acceptance of Bobby Brown, John gave his blessings. Maybe there was some money to be made with this raw kid. He began looking at his future son-in-law as a possible business venture. Bobby's career was faltering and John believed he could revive it. Maybe he would have better luck managing a man's career than he had with the two headstrong women in his life. He began a campaign to win over Bobby.

Bickering was at an all-time high among the Royal Family, and even Clive Davis joined the fray. He was worried about Bobby's bad-boy image and was afraid it would rub off on Whitney. Arista Records had spent millions of dollars and many years creating and polishing the image of their client as a wholesome, churchgoing sweetheart, and she was by far their most successful artist. Maintaining her status as superstar was more important than ever, and Davis shuddered that she might throw it all away on some lowlife from the 'hood. He called a meeting with her and asked for her personal guarantee that Bobby was ready to settle down.

Then Whitney's attorney called a meeting and presented her with a prenuptial agreement for Bobby to sign. She was insulted and told him so. Her man loved *her*, not her money. Regina said Cissy was furious that Whitney wouldn't take her attorney's advice. After all, she was now worth over $30 million and Cissy didn't want Bobby to get any of it.

The guest list kept growing, and when Whitney personally invited me, I told her nothing could keep me away. She said she would send me an invitation and told me to hang on to it because they would have so much security no one would be allowed in without one. I promised to guard it with my life.

Later that night while Regina and I were having dinner, she asked me, "Kevin, if someone offered you five thousand dollars for your wedding invitation, would you sell it?"

"Hell, no," I said. "I promised Whitney I'd be there and nothing could keep me away." I was curious and asked her why she had asked such a question.

"I've been getting dozens of calls from the press. Everybody wants a copy of the invitation to run in their paper." She laughed and said, "It looks like little Nippy is the hottest ticket in town these days."

Several days later I asked Regina when I could expect my invitation, and she said they were being delivered three days before the wedding for security reasons. I didn't think anything of it until I was passing a newsstand one day and saw Whitney's picture on the cover of the *Globe* with a blurb about her wedding invitation. I bought the paper and inside was a copy of her "official wedding invitation" as well as information on what kind of gown she would be wearing. The very first thought to come into my mind was, of course, Regina. I just knew she had something to do with this.

When I got back to her place, I showed her the paper and she shrugged and said, "That's a phony. The real invitations are being handmade and the designer is still working on them."

I believed her, but a couple of days later I caught her. It was Sunday morning and she thought I was still asleep, but I had gotten up for something and as I walked past the kitchen entrance, I saw her standing on a stool, placing a folder on the top of a cabinet. I pretended I hadn't seen anything and she soon left to meet her mother at church.

I took down the folder and opened it. It was stuffed full of copies of stories she had sold to the tabloids on everyone from Whitney to Michael Jackson, Oprah Winfrey, and many other stars. There were photocopies of the checks she had received, and the amount was staggering. No wonder she was able to live like a queen in this luxurious apartment in the best part of town! And there was Whitney's wedding invitation.

I went through all her papers and discovered she had a sophisticated underground operation. Many of her sources came from the office of the *Chicago Sun Times* columnist Irving "Kup" Kupcinet. Kup received wires from all over the world for his column, and someone would pick them up and send them on to Regina, who would then sell them to the tabloids. I found information on Stedman Graham, Oprah Winfrey's boyfriend. Regina had known him for many years, and every time they spoke, she would weasel little bits of information out of him regarding Oprah, then changing the story just enough so he wouldn't recognize where it came from, she would sell it to the rags.

Looking back, I was just as big a whore as she was. I wanted stardom more than anything and I was convinced Regina was my ticket to the Houston family and their support.

When she came home, I was sitting on the sofa, holding the folder, and she started cussing and screaming, saying, "How dare you go through my personal belongings," and she started to slap me, but I grabbed her arm. "You're sick," I said. "You need help. How could you do this to Whitney? She's always treated you right and paid you a good salary. Why would you do something like this? Just tell me why."

"I need money," she said sullenly. "I have a lot of bills and I also help my mother out. You know that."

It was true. I had seen her give her mother checks from time to time, but certainly nowhere near this much. "Your greed is going to be your downfall," I told her. "You've betrayed too many people and your karma is going to catch up to you." I felt sick to my stomach knowing I loved a woman who could be so devious, and I wanted to get as far away from her as possible. "You know," I said, "it's not just the stories, but how could you sell Whitney's wedding invitation? That's low, man. That really sucks."

I was walking toward the door and I said, more to myself than to her, "I've got half a mind to tell Whitney what you did."

She came flying across the room and threw herself on me, wrapping her arms and legs around me, crying and pleading with me not to tell Whitney. "Please, Kevin, please, baby," she sobbed. "Don't do this. I'll change, I promise. Give me another chance, please, baby."

She started kissing me and rubbing herself against me, reaching down to grip and stroke my penis. I felt myself weakening as I always did when she turned on her special brand of lovemaking. This day was no different as I allowed myself to be led to her bedroom.

As the wedding date drew closer, tensions at Nippy, Inc. were exploding all over. The woman who had just given birth to Bobby's baby called constantly, threatening to disrupt the wedding and "destroy Whitney Houston" if she didn't call it off.

Robyn had tried everything she could think of to break up Bobby and Whitney, but it wasn't working. Then John Houston approached me and said he'd be willing to pay "big money to have somebody blow Robyn away." Then he changed it to "just busting her up good, breaking a few bones and teaching the interfering bitch to mind her own business. If I had her killed, it would break Nippy's heart."

Robyn was freaking out all the time, bad-mouthing Bobby, saying what a womanizing, low-life druggie he was, and she wasn't going to let Whitney throw her life away by marrying him. She verbally attacked everyone at Nippy, Inc. who didn't agree with her, and finally Whitney called a halt. They actually came to blows and Whitney kicked her out of her New Jersey mansion, where Robyn had been living for years. Bobby was now spending most of his time there, and on more than one occasion he had told Robyn he wasn't about to share his house with her after he and Whitney were married. "And I'm not sharing my wife with you either, so get used to it!" Bobby asserted.

Someone leaked the feuding to the tabloids (I wonder who!), creating all kinds of speculation about Whitney's lesbian lover being ousted in favor of bad boy Bobby Brown. With her wedding just around the corner, Whitney realized that she would have to try, once again, to prove that she was a heterosexual woman marrying the man she loved. She spoke with a reporter from the *Los Angeles Times,* claiming, "Robyn is my best friend, who knows me better than any woman has ever known me. We have been tight for years, but when I met Bobby, Robyn and I had had enough time together. We used to be roommates, but now that I'm getting married, she moved into her own place, about thirty minutes away."

A couple of weeks before the wedding, Robyn did a complete about-face. She was warm and friendly and seemed to accept that Whitney was no longer in her life. She called Regina and suggested they give Whitney a shower at the Rihga Royal Hotel in Manhattan. It was quite a star-studded party with champagne, caviar, and lots of laughs. "Whitney had a great time," Regina told me. "She got a lot of sexy undies and nightgowns, and somebody gave her a pair of velvet handcuffs and a glow-in-the-dark condom. But she won't be needing the condom. She told me she wants to get pregnant as soon as possible."

Robyn's good mood lasted until the shower was over, then she was back to bad-mouthing Bobby to everyone who would listen. Bobby felt the same way about Robyn as she felt about him, and they tried to stay out of each other's way for Whitney's sake. But with a wedding to plan it was difficult. One night a group of them were sitting around after dinner discussing the wedding when Bobby told Robyn he wanted to get a couple of things off his chest. He didn't like the fact that Whitney and Robyn often shared each other's clothes, and he told her he didn't like to see her wearing his woman's clothes. *Star* magazine had just come out with an item that probably triggered this confrontation.

According to Janet Carlton writing in *Star,* Whitney and Robyn were seen shopping together at Barneys in New York. "They picked out an armload of men's clothes and the clerk assumed they were for Bobby, but Whitney said, 'No, I want to try them on.' She and Robyn tried men's suits, jackets, and shoes and ended up buying identical men's Dolce & Gabbana sweaters."

Robyn, ever pugnacious, took offense at Bobby's opinion about the clothes sharing and jumped to her feet, jabbing her finger in his face. The argument soon escalated into a shouting match with Robyn taking a swing at him. Whitney grabbed her, pulling her off and leading her away while stunned guests stared in disbelief.

Later Whitney laughed it off, telling a reporter, "Of course that's not true! First of all, if it were true, Robyn would have been knocked out. But Bobby is a gentleman. He would never fight a woman." The guests who had witnessed the tussle just shook their heads and laid bets on how long this marriage would last—or even if it would take place.

People who had known Whitney for years were seeing a change come over her. She had become more brittle, testy, and short-tempered. She had always hated reporters, but now they just seemed to amuse her. She didn't seem to care what they wrote about her. "They're gonna write what they fuckin' well please, anyway," she said to me and Regina one day. "It don't matter what I say. They just make up some shit and say I said it."

I noticed something else about her, too. She started to talk in the hard-edged slang of a street tough, very ethnic and confrontational. She swaggered when she walked, and if she was wearing jeans, she would hook her thumbs through the belt loops like a guy.

"People think I'm Miss Prissy Pooh-Pooh," she told a reporter for *Time* magazine. "But I'm not. I like to have fun. I can get down, really freakin' dirty with you. I can get raunchy. I've learned to be freer just being with Bobby. I've learned to be a little more loose—not so contained, ya know? Since I've been with him, I've gotten, you know, a little bit freer with my shit."

Bobby told the *Los Angeles Times,* "I may be a bad boy and she may be America's Sweetheart, but it's love. When it happens, you have to grab it. You can't let it go no matter what anybody else thinks. Whitney is a proud black woman. That's what really drew me to her. She's beautiful, not just outside, but on the inside. When we finish a show, she puts on jeans and we roll."

Wedding gifts were pouring in, paintings, crystal, jewelry, silver, kitchen appliances. Regina would open them and keep the presents she wanted, then forward the rest to Whitney. When I told her she was stealing like a common thief, she told me to mind my own business.

Bobby was still generating bad press, due to a public drunkenness charge, and Whitney's fans were scolding her publicly with signs that read "Whitney, how could you?" and "Don't marry him, Whitney."

Whitney responded, "I'm like this American princess and white America wants me to marry a white guy. They don't understand why I'd want a strong black man."

Bobby's longtime friend Jamie Foster Brown (no relation), publisher of *Sister 2 Sister,* came to his rescue and told the press,

"A lot of men are threatened by strong and powerful women, but not Bobby. He always supported Whitney. She knows the private side of Bobby, a side the public doesn't know. I know he's wild and gotten out of hand recently, but I also know he's a kind, sensitive, and humble man who loves to cook and loves Whitney and loves all his children. All kinds of women have been throwing themselves at him since he was thirteen years old. Most men, especially artists, aren't equipped to say no. But Whitney vows that doesn't matter; she believes he will evolve. White people don't understand how hard it is for a successful black woman to find a black man she can be an equal with. I'm telling you, there are not a lot of options out there!"

In turn, Robyn's behavior was so bizarre it had everyone in the Houston family worried. She would throw temper tantrums daily, threatening to kick everybody's ass, cussing people out right and left, and making the staff at Nippy, Inc. feel miserable. She told me, Regina, and John, "If Whitney goes through with this marriage, I'll hold a press conference and tell everyone I'm Whitney's lover, that we've been lovers for years, then I'll kill myself!"

She was constantly telling us that she was going to sell to the press the story about her relationship with Whitney and everyone at Nippy, Inc. She claimed to have information about a drug deal involving Bobby Brown, and she was going to phone the police.

John was at his wit's end. He had tried everything he could to quiet Robyn, but she was out of control and continued to stir up trouble wherever she went. Finally, he approached me and said, "We've got to do something about that motherfucking bitch. She's ruining my family and driving everybody nuts. She's always controlled Whitney, and now that she can't anymore, she's losing her grip on reality. I'm seriously afraid she's going to hurt somebody. We can't let that happen, Kevin. I won't let anything happen to Nippy.

"I'd like to just blow the motherfucking dyke's head off, but if I did, it would kill Whitney. I don't want to lose my baby."

We talked for quite a while and finally he came to the point.

I'll pay you six thousand dollars if you put the fear of God in her. Beat the shit out of her, break a few bones so she'll know I mean business."

"I have a problem with that, John," I said slowly. I couldn't believe he was serious. I was stalling, trying to see what else he had to say. "How could I get that close? She knows me and—"

He interrupted with a wave of his hand and another string of obscenities. "Come up behind her and hit her over the head with a baseball bat. Then put her legs over the curb and smash 'em, break her kneecaps and both her arms!"

He raved on for several more minutes, and I was shaking my head, saying, "No, John. Hey, man, I can't do that—"

"I'll get you a record deal. I promise, you'll have an album out by the end of the month. You've got to do this for me, Kevin."

Needless to say, I passed. On the way home from his place, I got another lesson in ruthlessness. Regina asked why I wouldn't attack Robyn. "It's no big deal," she said. "You'd be doing everybody a favor, and you also would have a record deal out of it. Why did you turn John down? I'd kill that fucking dyke in a minute if I thought I could get away with it. But everybody knows how much I hate her, so they'd know I did it."

When we got back to the apartment, I noticed three beautiful statues sitting on Regina's table. I asked her where they had come from, and she said they had been sent to Whitney, but she liked them so much she had decided to keep them for herself. "They're Lladro—from Spain," she told me, "and they're very, very expensive."

"Regina, that's the same as stealing," I said. "How can you do that to Whitney?"

"It's not stealing because Whitney will never know. She has no idea of what people send to her."

It was now three days before the wedding and I still hadn't received my invitation. When I questioned Regina about it, she put me off with vague promises that "it was on its way," but I was starting to worry. I wanted to go to this wedding more than

109

anything in the world. I had seen a copy of the guest list, and it read like a who's who of Hollywood greats. Eight hundred people were invited, but I can only remember a few of them, my all-time favorite celebrities such as Stevie Wonder (who Regina later told me also performed at the reception), Leslie Uggams, Patti LaBelle, Dionne Warwick, Aretha Franklin, Gladys Knight, Natalie Cole—all longtime friends and fellow black performers. What really threw me was to discover that Donald Trump and Marla Maples were going! I didn't even how Whitney knew them.

At about this time I did something really stupid. Regina said Whitney was a nervous wreck about all the stories in the tabloids about Bobby's drug-dealing ways, and she was afraid to buy any pot. She wanted to know if I'd bring her some the next time I flew in. "Besides, she thinks the weed from Chicago is better, more potent," Regina said.

I would have done anything for Whitney by this time, so, like a fool, I agreed. I stuffed an ounce of marijuana down into my underwear and went to the airport. I was sweating like crazy, afraid some drug-sniffing dog would go after me. I can't tell you how nervous I was during that entire trip, and I vowed I would never take such a foolish chance again. So the next time Regina approached me, telling me Whitney wanted me to bring her some weed, I turned her down flat. There's no way I would jeopardize my freedom and face a possible prison term, not even for Whitney Houston.

Late afternoon, July 17, the day before the wedding, I had to face the fact that I wouldn't be there. My invitation never arrived, and I couldn't get Regina on the phone. It was obvious even to the biggest fool in the world what had happened. The copy of the invitation I'd seen in the *Globe* had been mine. Regina had intercepted it and sold it to them. It broke my heart. It was the most devastating disappointment of my life.

10

Hustling Wedding Pictures

ON JULY 18, 1992, THE DIVA OF POP AND THE BAD BOY OF R&B exchanged vows. The nuptials were held in Whitney's multi-million-dollar New Jersey mansion. The New York Metropolitan Opera's seventeen-piece orchestra played the wedding march as John Houston walked his Nippy down the flower-strewn aisle.

As reported by Jeffrey Bowman in his book *Diva*, "Guests gasped at Whitney's stunning wedding gown. The $30,000 gown, made of French Lyon lace with iridescent beads, white pearls and sequins, trailed to the floor. Its front was a bodice cut, with soft lace covering Whitney's neck and shoulders, leading to a pearl choker with drop beads. The gown featured a four-foot train—the lace alone costing over $4,000. Whitney wore a matching, beaded skull-cap, to which a veil had been attached. Simple, white, low-heeled shoes ensured that she did not appear taller than her husband.

"Bobby, who seemed extremely nervous, wore a white suit with tails. His shirt was cowl-collard, clasped at the throat with a silver jewel."

Regina told me she had never seen Whitney looking more beautiful or happy. "I'm beginning to believe that she's really *in love* with this kid," she said. "They couldn't keep their hands or eyes off each other. As soon as the preacher declared them man and wife, seven white doves were released and flew overhead. It was the most magnificent wedding in the world."

Then Regina cuddled against me and said in a tiny little voice, "I wish you could have been there, baby. I'm just heartsick about your invitation getting lost."

I leaned my head back on the sofa and closed my eyes as she chattered on about the wedding and reception. I guess hearing about it from someone who'd been there was better than nothing.

She said Whitney had hired a whole army of security guards, and the guests had to go through a metal detector and five checkpoints to enter. Bodyguards stood in front of the bridal party at all times. "Whitney didn't know it," Regina said, "but John had hired his own bodyguards to keep an eye on Robyn. He was afraid she'd carry out her many threats to kill Bobby. He said, 'That bitch is just crazy enough to try and pull some stunt like that,' and he wasn't taking any chances on Nippy getting hurt."

Regina was surprised and a little miffed that Whitney had chosen Robyn as her maid of honor because *she* wanted to stand up with the bride. "I would've thought she'd want a *woman* as her maid of honor instead of some nasty old dyke."

She told me that on the morning of the wedding, Whitney had a black Porsche delivered to Robyn's house to ensure that she would be in a good mood and not cause a scene or embarrass her. The press reported that the Porsche was a gift of appreciation for Robyn's many years of loyalty.

Regina screamed with laughter, rolling all over the bed and saying, "More like many years of ass-kissin' and pussy-eatin'."

No cameras had been allowed at the wedding except those of the official photographer, Marc Murphy Bryant, whom Whitney had hired. Before leaving on her honeymoon, she told Regina to sell some of the photos to the *National Enquirer* and give John Houston the money. In case of an emergency, she also told

Regina where she and Bobby were planning to go on their honeymoon and swore her to secrecy. They would be away for two weeks, and Whitney needed a vacation away from prying eyes and the stress of the past few months. She didn't want anyone to disturb her plans, especially not the paparazzi.

After partying until dawn with their guests, the bride and groom flew aboard the Concorde to Europe, where a yacht would be waiting to take them on a ten-day Mediterranean cruise. The 140-foot yacht had a crew of nine and was equipped with everything the newlyweds would need—Jacuzzi, TV, VCR, stereo—all paid for by Arista and MCA Records.

"Pretty classy wedding gift," Regina said when she told me about it. "Not that they can't afford it. Whitney's made them millions of dollars." Everything was about money with Regina.

The very next day, Regina started wheeling and dealing. She knew John Houston was expecting $15,000 so she started wrangling with the tabloids, seeing who would pay the most. She made a deal for $85,000 plus an additional $2,500 for the whereabouts of the honeymoon. Now all she had to do was get her hands on the negatives and have copies made. No one would be the wiser. She would pay John his $15,000 and make a tidy little profit for herself. Before Whitney left, she told Regina she wanted Robyn to go with Regina to pick up the pictures at noon on Monday.

Robyn had long suspected Regina was the leak at Nippy, Inc., but Whitney had not believed her. However, to keep Robyn appeased, Whitney agreed that she would go with Regina to get the photographs and negatives from Marc Bryant—just in case.

Regina called Marc Bryant on Sunday and told him some story about her needing to pick up "a few photos later on today, then Robyn and I will come by tomorrow for the rest of them." Marc had taken literally hundreds of pictures so this was no problem, and he innocently let Regina have her pick.

In the meantime, John called and asked Regina if he could see the pictures first as he wanted some for his "own personal album," when all along *he* had cut his own deal with another

113

tabloid in London! Everybody had an agenda, including Robyn. *She* wanted to see the pictures first as she had made an arrangement with Johnson Publications for an exclusive photo of Bobby and Whitney, and she had also promised to send some to *Ebony* magazine.

Regina had planned on arriving at Marc's studio before Robyn and replacing the photos she had copied, but Robyn arrived early and, going through the photographs, noticed that several were missing. Robyn was livid and demanded to know what Regina was doing with the pictures. Innocently, Regina told her John had wanted to take a look at them before they were sent to the *Enquirer*. "See, here they are. What's the problem?"

Regina called me (she had spent the last three days at Whitney's estate in New Jersey) and told me Robyn gave her the coldest, hardest, most hateful look she had ever seen. Then Robyn said, "I know what you're up to, Regina, and this time you're not going to get away with it."

"I swear to God, Kevin, I got cold chills. It felt like a witch was walking over my grave."

I picked Regina up at the airport that night and we hadn't been in her condo more than three minutes when Robyn called. Regina answered, listened for a couple of seconds, then went ballistic, screaming at the top of her lungs, "Drop dead, you fucking dyke! I don't have to listen to your shit!" She slammed the receiver down and it rang again immediately. She snatched it up and yelled, "I'm not afraid of your motherfuckin' ass, you sick dyke! Just wait until Whitney gets back, you're going to be in a whole shitful of trouble!" She slammed the receiver down once more and it started ringing again, so this time I answered, figuring I had better put an end to this.

"She's just pissed off because Whitney wants to lead a normal life," Regina was yelling. "Damn, stupid dyke—I wish she'd just drop dead and give everybody a break!"

When Robyn heard my voice, she said, "I'm sorry you're mixed up with that bitch, Kevin, because she's in big trouble. Tell her for me her days at Nippy, Inc. are numbered. I've always suspected she was the one feeding the rags, and now I know it. You can also tell her she's a low-down, double-crossing cunt and I can't wait to see her head roll when Whitney gets home."

I didn't have a chance to say a word before Regina ripped the phone out of the wall and threw it clear across the room. She was sobbing hysterically and kept saying, "I didn't do anything wrong—I just did what Whitney told me to do. I sold the pictures to the *Enquirer* and I'm going to give the money to John, just like Whitney said."

I suggested she call John and tell him what had just transpired with Robyn. "If you were following Whitney's orders," I said, "there shouldn't by any problem." I knew about her deal for the $85,000—plus the additional $2,500 for the honeymoon plans—but she didn't know I knew. I couldn't wait to see how she planned to wiggle out of this one. She was a master manipulator, so I poured myself a glass of wine and leaned back to watch an artist at work.

She put the phone back together and plugged it into the jack and dialed John's number. Her hands were shaking. I'd never seen her this upset before, but I didn't feel the least bit sorry for her. This showdown had been coming for a long time. She explained to John what had happened with Robyn and told him, "I didn't do anything wrong, John. I was following Whitney's orders. I have a check for you in my purse for fifteen thousand dollars."

"Made out to me?" John asked. "In my name?" When Regina said yes, he said, "That was very stupid, Regina. You know I can't have no checks made out to me. The tabloids can trace it back to Whitney. She probably meant for you to cut a cash deal or have the check made out to someone else."

Regina told me every time someone at Nippy, Inc. sold a story to the tabloids, they would have the check made out to someone outside the Royal Family, usually one of Whitney's aunts. John asked to speak to me, and when I got on the phone, he told me his attorney, Sheldon Platt, was on the other line so he would be listening to what we said.

"Regina really fucked up this time," John said. "Whitney is going to be furious when she gets home. It will look real bad if the public thinks she's selling her own wedding pictures to one of those trashy rags. So I need you to do me a favor. Will you go to Florida [where the *Enquirer* had its office] and exchange the check for another one, made out to Ellen White? Regina can't go into the office now because they'll be able to trace it back to Nippy." Ellen White is a very close friend of the family and they've used her name in the past, giving her a few dollars when a check is made out to her.

He offered to pay all my expenses so I said, "Sure, John, I'll do this for you."

Regina called editor John South of the *National Enquirer*, and he agreed to exchange the check, so we were on our way.

We stayed at the Ocean Grand Hotel in West Palm Beach. We hadn't been in our room for more than a few minutes when John Houston called, screaming and cussing. He said Robyn had informed him about the double cross Regina had pulled with the wedding pictures. Apparently, the Associated Press and Johnson Publications had exclusive rights to the pictures and a signed deal with Robyn. If any photos appeared in any other publication, they could and most likely *would* sue Nippy, Inc. John Houston ordered Regina to call John South and cancel the deal, return the check, and get back to Chicago.

Now Regina was really anxious. It had to be the hardest call she had ever made, but she got South on the phone and explained there had been a "mix-up and a misunderstanding," and she was sorry, but she had to cancel the deal with the *Enquirer*.

South said it was too late to back out, it was a done deal, and she started begging and pleading with him to please give her a break. "My job's on the line," she told him. "I have to get out of this deal or I'm going to be in a lot of trouble."

He said he was sorry but it was too late; she could do nothing now except exchange the check made out to John for the one made out to Ellen White. The next morning I went to South's office and made the exchange, and we caught the next flight back to Chicago. Regina didn't say more than a dozen words. She was depressed and scared, thinking about what would happen to her job. John Houston now knew all about the $85,000 plus the $2,500 for the honeymoon plans, and he was ready to confront her next time he saw her. We found out later he had talked to South personally and discovered Regina's shenanigans. He had also talked to Robyn and found out about the photographs Regina had had copied.

When we got back to the apartment, there was a message from John ordering Regina to be at Nippy, Inc. first thing in the morning for a meeting. She begged me to go with her. She was afraid of what John and Robyn would do to her. "They're gonna kick my ass," she kept saying, and she was crying and pleading with me to please go with her and protect her.

"You got yourself into this mess," I told her, "and you're going to have to get yourself out. How many times have I told you that I didn't condone what you've been doing to Whitney? You let greed get the best of you. All you ever think about is money, and you don't care who you hurt as long as you get paid."

The next morning I was visiting my mother when my beeper went off. It was an emergency 911 page from Regina, calling from the office. I returned the call and she was hysterical, crying so hard I could hardly understand her. "That fucking dyke tried to kill me," she said. "She attacked me and choked me and my neck is bleeding! I told you this would happen. I begged you to come with me, but you wouldn't."

I managed to calm her down and she said Robyn had jumped on her, knocking her to the floor and trying to choke her. When John tried to pull her off, she slapped his face and started beating on him, too. I was sick of all the violence around me. I had never seen such a bunch of volatile people and I wished I could just walk away from them all. But they kept dangling that carrot in front of me, promising me a record contract, and I still wanted to believe them. I had a gut feeling Regina would be fired when Whitney returned from her honeymoon, and I was right.

Regina called me from the offices of Nippy, Inc. and she was furious. "I just got fired," she said. "John's still here and I told him that was the biggest mistake he and Whitney ever made! I'm sick of this bullshit and I'm gonna blow the lid off this fucking place." She was talking loud, more to John than to me. "I'm glad this happened. I can make more money writing a book than I ever did here. I'm gonna tell the world about Miss Goody-Goody being a dyke, and I'm gonna tell about John trying to solicit you to beat up Robyn. I was there, remember? I heard every fucking word."

I heard John's voice in the background saying, "That would be a very, very big mistake, Regina."

I told her I would meet her at the airport and we'd talk about it then.

As soon as we got back home, she lit into me, blaming me for losing her job. "If you'd just done what John asked you to and beat the shit out of that dyke, I'd still be working for Whitney. He didn't ask you to kill her, for God's sake, just put her ass in the hospital for a few months. I bet she wouldn't be so damn quick to tell stories about me if she had a busted jaw!"

The next few days were terrible as Regina continued to rant and rave and tell everyone she was going to write the hottest exposé about the Royal Family. "And I know where all the bodies are buried," she said. John and Cissy both called several times, pleading with Regina to "give up this foolish idea and calm down long enough for us to have a serious talk." Cissy asked her if she would feel better if she received severance pay and said Nippy, Inc. was willing to pay her well for her years of service if she would stop threatening to write a book.

Then Whitney called and Regina listened for a few seconds, then said, "It's a little late for apologies now. You don't give a fuck about me. You're just scared that I'm going to write a book and tell the world what you're *really* like." They spoke for a few minutes with Regina becoming belligerent and cussing her out, then slamming down the phone. It rang a second later, and when I answered, Whitney said, "Kevin, put Regina on the phone."

Regina refused to speak to her and Whitney said to me, "Kevin, you better talk to her crazy ass and tell her she's fucking with the wrong person. Nobody's going to talk to me like that or threaten me and my family. And tell her for me she's a low-down, double-crossing bitch."

The rest of the week John and Cissy phoned daily to try to talk some sense into Regina. At one point Cissy even offered to try to get Regina's job back for her, but Regina said, "Shove it—I wouldn't work for her again for no amount of money!"

Cissy pleaded with her to please take the severance check and leave them alone. She said Whitney was pregnant and all this turmoil wasn't good for her. Cissy was trying everything in her power to calm Regina down, but John was another story. He said to me, "Kevin, you tell that crazy bitch if she writes a book, she won't live long enough to read it!"

An offer was then made of $500,000 if Regina would sign a disclaimer, and she told them, "Shit, man, I got an offer from a publisher for more than that—and once the book comes out, I'll make millions!"

Whitney called and told Regina if she wrote a book, Whitney would sue her for every cent she had.

Regina was constantly plotting how to get back at the Houstons for the way they were treating her. I tried many times to talk some sense into her, and I urged her to take the severance pay and get on with her life, but she refused. No way would she sign a disclaimer. I reminded her that Whitney was pregnant and this was supposed to be a happy time, not one filled with so much stress. She just said, "Fuck her—and fuck you, too, if you're not going to support me in this."

That's when I packed my bags and went back to my wife and family.

11

Feuding in the Royal Family

LATE SUMMER AND EARLY FALL OF 1992 WERE HARD ON WHITNEY. She was sick a lot during the early stages of her pregnancy, and having Regina add more stress with her threats and constant hostility did not help matters. *The Bodyguard* was set for release, and Whitney had to return to the studio and polish up the vocals that were used in the movie. She sang six songs in the movie, and they had to choose one for the theme. Kevin Costner suggested "I Will Always Love You," and Whitney thought it was a perfect choice.

Clive Davis and producer-arranger David Foster weren't convinced, however. They wanted something a little more upbeat and suggested "I'm Every Woman," but Costner prevailed. He also insisted that Whitney open the song singing a cappella. Nobody else liked the arrangement, but again, what Costner wanted, Costner got. And he proved to be right. It became a number one megahit, staying on top of the charts a unprecedented fourteen weeks—the longest-running number one song in the history of the *Billboard* charts.

When reporters asked Dolly Parton what she thought of her song's becoming such a huge success as performed by Whitney, she just grinned and replied, "Honey, every time that record is played it means more money in my pocket. I'm tickled to death!" To this date, she's earned about $3 million on the release.

Whitney's career had never been healthier and she had never been happier. She loved being married and pregnant. She pooh-poohed all the rumors that Bobby was still up to his womanizing ways, telling *Vibe* magazine, "I've got a *good* man. He takes care of me. I don't have to be scared of anything because I know he will kick ass. Disrespect him and you've got a problem."

Bobby's once-promising career had hit a snag and his newly released album was a disappointment. His finances were floundering and he was on the verge of losing his home in Atlanta when his new bride came to the rescue. The IRS had tax liens of $1.3 million on his Tudor-style mansion when Nippy, Inc. bought it at auction. It was badly neglected, obviously the target of vandals, with doors hanging off their hinges, toilets overflowing, and snakes slithering across the bottom of the empty swimming pool.

Bobby was on the verge of becoming Mr. Houston and it bothered him. Always combative, he became even more surly with reporters and always traveled with "his boys" as backup security. He was embarrassed that his album had been a failure and his career was failing while his wife's continued to soar. The drug rumors continued to follow him, and when Cissy walked in on "his boys" doing lines of cocaine in Whitney's kitchen, she threatened to call the police. Hardly a week went by without the tabloids reporting on some new fracas in which Bobby was involved. He and Whitney were seen arguing in public on several occasions, prompting reports that the marriage was already in trouble. Whitney laughed and shrugged it off. "We don't just have arguments," she said. "We have good ol' knock-down, drag-

'em-out *married people* fights. Ooooh, he makes me so mad. He has a temper from hell, but I love him so."

The Bodyguard premiered on November 23, 1992, at Grummann's Chinese Theater in Hollywood and was attended by show business's glittering elite. It was panned by critics but completely embraced by the moviegoing public. Everyone, it seemed, was clamoring to get a look at Whitney Houston up there on the silver screen, and they weren't disappointed; she'd never looked more beautiful. (The movie went on to earn over $400 million worldwide while the sound track sold 33 million copies and became a number one hit.) Three of the songs in the album, "I'm Every Woman," "Queen of the Night," and "I Have Nothing," would also become huge hits, proving once again that Whitney had multimedia clout.

The public may have loved Whitney, but they didn't feel the same way about her husband. "What does she see in him?" reporters would ask in every article written about the newlyweds. Nobody could understand why she continued to stand up for her man even as he continued his bad behavior, but she did. On his album, titled simply *Bobby*, she joined him in a duet, "Something in Common," and Bobby dedicated the song to "all those who don't believe in love, especially ours."

Whitney was hoping that her singing on Bobby's album would help make it a success, but it was poorly received and sales were disappointing. Obviously this caused conflict in the marriage as Bobby began to think he was forever doomed to be compared to his famous wife. He had always been ambitious and had worked for many years to become a success, now he wasn't sure it would ever happen.

Christmas of 1992 was a solemn affair for the Royal Family. The marriage was only five months old and it seemed to be straining at the seams. Whitney was hugely pregnant at almost two hundred pounds and was understandably uncomfortable. Having to deal with the press about her husband was bad enough, but her parents had still not accepted him, either. Ru-

123

mors that he was a crackhead persisted, and Cissy believed them. She was barely civil to her son-in-law, and Robyn Crawford was just as chilly toward him. He must have felt as if he were in a lion's den with those two strong-willed, domineering, and critical women.

Whitney was furious that magazines continued to speculate on her sexual preference. "I'm a married woman, for God's sake! A very pregnant married woman. I'm so fucking tired of answering the 'gay' question. When the hell are they going to leave me alone?"

Bobby's marriage to Whitney threw him into the spotlight as well, and he didn't like it any better than she did. "We are in love whether anyone believes it or not," he said. "I am not a junkie and my wife is not a lesbian, okay? I didn't marry her to further my career and she didn't marry me to stop the gay rumors. We fell in love, we got married, and we're having a bay, that's it." Never had a marriage come under such intense scrutiny, and it was driving them crazy.

During the holidays I got back together with Regina. We had continued to speak over the phone, and I was also still in touch with John and Cissy. With her job at Nippy, Inc. gone, Regina needed another position and asked me to help her. I called a friend of mine, Allen Johnson, at Joey Boy Records, who gave her a job as vice president of publicity. Her salary was $2,500 per month, and she was also doing publicity for the gospel group Comission, in Detroit, for $1,600 and for Walt Whitman and the Soul Children, for another $1,600. More than enough money for her to live quite comfortably, but she was still greedy and wanted more. She called me one day and said she had talked to the editor of *Globe* and told them about John Houston's soliciting me to beat up Robyn.

"They said they'd pay you fifty thousand dollars for your story," she told me, "and they want you to fly out to Los Angeles and meet with them."

At first I refused, but she assured me they wouldn't use my

name or picture, they just wanted the details of the story. They would pay for my time away from work and all my expenses, so I thought about it and agreed. It was cold in Chicago and a few days in sunny L.A. sounded good. Besides, I felt I should go public with what had transpired between John and me in case anything happened to me later on. He is a ruthless bastard and he's not used to anyone telling him no, so I was worried about what he might do. I was put up in a nice condo in Westwood and had a meeting with Kathy Tracy, a reporter for the *Globe,* who told me a very different story than Regina had. They wanted me to pose for photographs and they wanted to use my name.

"That's not what I was told," I said to Kathy. "I thought you just wanted to hear my story."

"We have to use your name and picture or we could be sued by John Houston. I told Ms. Brown what we needed."

Once again, Regina had lied to me. I was already thinking of backing out when Kathy insisted on a polygraph test, two in fact, administered by an ex–CIA agent. They asked lots of questions about Whitney's family and my dealings with them, and I passed. Now that they were sure my story was true, they really wanted to run it. I said, "Let me think about it and I'll call you later."

Back at the condo I called Regina and told her what had happened. "You know I don't want my name or picture being used," I said.

"Kevin, don't be an ass," she said. "Get the money. We're talking fifty grand here. So what if they want to use your name and picture. Big fucking deal. It'll blow over in a couple of weeks."

"No way," I told her, then I called Kathy Tracy to tell her I wasn't interested in doing the story. She told me that Regina had cut a deal with them for "compensation" for arranging the story with me, and Kathy tried to talk me into doing it.

On the plane traveling back to Chicago, I thought about what a mess my life had become because of Regina Brown, and I decided I was going to take charge again. John and Cissy were still being threatened with exposure in Regina's book, so I decided to change camps. When I got home, I would call John and tell him what I knew about Regina's manuscript and offer to thwart her plans. I knew her attorney, Linda Mensche, and had attended many meetings with them, and I thought I could probably get her to represent me.

When I left Regina right after the wedding, I'd been writing down every illegal thing she'd ever done to the Houstons and I had quite a hefty manuscript of my own. Regina is very protective of her reputation in the music business and would not want *anyone* to know how she really treats her clients. I figured if I could threaten her with an exposé, she would drop her own exposé against the Houstons and they would be grateful. On many occasions, both John and Whitney had promised me a record contract and that would be my "compensation"—I didn't want any money, I just wanted what they had promised me, a singing career.

I wrote John with my proposition as soon as I got home. I wanted everything to be in writing as I didn't trust anyone. I also got my manuscript together, made copies, and had it notarized on December 14, 1992. I met with Regina's attorney, Linda Mensche, and asked her what was happening with Regina's lawsuit, and she said Regina couldn't make up her mind what she wanted to do. One minute she said she wanted to go ahead with the book and the next minute she wanted to negotiate a deal with the Houstons for her severance pay, but she refused to sign a disclaimer.

I was having dinner with Regina one night and brought up the subject, telling her she should just take the severance pay John had offered and get on with her life.

"You're making everyone miserable with your hostile behavior," I told her. "If you keep this up, the Houstons are going to get so pissed, they won't give you anything."

"Fuck 'em," she said. "I'll make millions on this book."

"Think about Whitney. Whether you want to admit it or not, she was very good to you for many years. She doesn't need this kind of shit in her life, especially now that she's pregnant. I can understand how you feel about John. Hell, everyone knows he's a snake in the grass, but you can't hurt him without hurting Whitney."

"Who cares? Nobody gave a fuck when they hurt me. They just fired me and kicked my ass out!"

I tried to explain she had betrayed Whitney with her double-dealing, selling her wedding pictures and also the information about the honeymoon, but Regina didn't see anything wrong with that. She insisted that at least half the stuff written about Whitney in the tabloids came from Whitney herself, so why shouldn't she make a few bucks on her own? I reminded her of all the gifts she had stolen from Whitney and several other things she had done that were illegal.

"I really want to help you out," I told her, "and I'm willing to go to John and negotiate your severance pay, but you'll have to sign a disclaimer, promising you'll never write anything about the Houstons."

She laughed in my face, and that's when I took my own manuscript out of my briefcase. I had more copies at home because I knew she would try to destroy it if she got her hands on it. "This is it, baby. Either you make a deal with the Houstons or I'll publish my own book exposing you as a thief and a liar. I don't think you want that. Your reputation will be destroyed in the music business. You won't be able to get a job working for Tiny Tim."

"You're bluffing," she said, but I saw fear in her eyes as it dawned on her all the things I'd been privy to in the past few years.

A couple of days later, John called me and said how much he appreciated what I was trying to do. "This shit that Regina is pulling is killing me and making Nippy a nervous wreck. She don't need to be worrying about that conniving little bitch while she's pregnant. She's got enough trouble with the media as it is. I would have taken care of the bitch myself, but I've been pretty sick lately."

He has diabetes, his eyesight was failing, and he wasn't as intimidating as he had once been. He had no problem with helping me get started in the business and said, "With all this shit going on, I forgot all about your music career, but if you can shut that bitch up, we'll get the ball rolling."

He asked me to fly to New Jersey to meet with him and to bring my manuscript. Donna, Michael's wife, who worked in the offices of Nippy, Inc., made my reservations. During the flight I fantasized about how happy and grateful everyone would be that I had gotten Regina off their backs. I just *knew* Whitney would make good on her promise of managing my career. After all the crap I'd been through with the Royal Family, I deserved it.

I checked into the Holiday Inn and went downstairs to wait for John in the bar. It was three days before Christmas and I was thinking what a terrific Christmas gift this would be. I did feel a little twinge of guilt about Regina, but I pushed it away. All the trouble she was having, she had brought on herself, and she had almost destroyed me in the process. It was time I started thinking about myself. I was sitting at the bar having a rum and Coke when I saw John walk in flanked on either side by a couple of white guys. I walked over and greeted him and he stared right into my eyes with a look of pure hatred. He didn't say a word.

One of the men extended his hand to me and said, "Hi, Kevin. I'm Sheldon Platt, Whitney's attorney." He introduced me to the other man, also an attorney, and John continued staring at me as if I were a piece of shit stuck to the bottom of his shoe. The silence grew until Mr. Platt said, "I have to apologize for John. He's been under the weather lately. This business with Ms. Brown is very stressful for everyone."

I ignored him and looked John straight in the eye. "I don't know what your problem is, but I don't like your attitude, John. I came all this way to try and help you out of a sticky situation, and you cop an attitude with me. I don't need this shit. You show me some respect or I'll take my happy ass back to Chicago!"

That got his attention and he said, "Kevin, I'm sorry. I'm truly sorry. It's not your fault. I've been sicker than a dog and I just want to get this over with as soon as possible. I don't want no lawsuits hanging over us when Whitney has her baby."

I congratulated him on becoming a granddaddy and he smiled for the first time. We went to the conference room and Platt said John had told him about my manuscript listing all the things Regina had done while working for Nippy, Inc. and could he see it. I had no problem with that; I'd brought it along for that reason, but now I was getting suspicious. John had led me to believe that we'd be signing a record-management deal, and when I saw the lawyers, I just assumed they were there with a contract.

"I've got it right here," I said, indicating my briefcase. "But I thought we were here to discuss my career. Why do these guys need to see the manuscript?"

"That's why *you* are here, Kevin," John said, "but the lawyers need to just take a look and see what we're talking about here."

I didn't need to feel a draft to know when somebody was blowing smoke up my ass.

The other attorney stepped in. "We need to know what Regina did, illegally, while working for Ms. Houston. And it's our intention to prosecute her."

"Damn right," John yelled. "I want to throw her ass in jail for all the pain and misery she's caused my family." He began ranting about what a double-crossing bitch she was and how she had been sleeping with at least a dozen other guys while living with me. He was like a toothless old lion, still roaring but nobody paid any attention to him. While one of the lawyers tried to calm him down, the other one was grilling me about Regina's book. He wanted to know if I'd seen it, and when I said I had, he asked me to tell him what I'd read.

"I won't do that," I told them. "I thought the purpose of this meeting was to stop her from publishing the book, not get her sent to jail."

They offered to pay for the information and asked me how much it would take to also see my manuscript. "It's not about money," I said. "It's never been about money. I want the Houstons to make good on their promise to get me a record deal. That's all I've ever wanted."

They continued to badger me and told me, "We're prepared to make you a very wealthy young man. All you have to do is tell us what you know about Ms. Brown's book and let us see what you've written."

I looked into John's eyes and a wave of fear washed over me. I actually felt goose bumps break out on my arms. Something was definitely wrong here. I was being set up. I mumbled something about having "to think it over," and I rushed back to my room and called Regina. No matter how many times she'd lied to me and screwed me over, I was still in love with her. I couldn't help myself. My only reason for making a deal with John was to stop Regina from writing a book and to pressure him into honoring our agreement regarding my music career. I did not want to be responsible for having her arrested or thrown in jail.

After I related what had transpired in the meeting, Regina asked if I had shown them the manuscript and I told her I hadn't.

I told her my flight was for the next day, and she said she would make arrangements for me to leave within the hour. "Just get the hell out of there and don't tell anyone you're leaving!"

I grabbed my bags and went straight to the airport, feeling as if I'd just escaped a really close call. I wasn't cut out for this cloak-and-dagger stuff. Ever since becoming involved with the Houstons, my life had been turned upside down.

Regina was waiting for me at the airport and threw herself into my arms, kissing me and crying and telling me how much she had missed me. We were ripping each other's clothes off the second we got home and fell into bed, promising never to part again. I felt a kinship with her as we were both victims of John Houston's wrath. We were also fellow conspirators in a way, and it brought us closer together.

In January 1993, Robyn called me. We hadn't spoken for a while so I was surprised to hear from her. Her voice was soft and a little sad when she said, "Hey, Kevin, how are you, baby?" We exchanged pleasantries for a few seconds, then she said, "I've heard some rumors around the office that really disturb me and I want to know if they're true. Did John offer to pay you to beat me up, to break my legs and arms?"

I didn't want to admit it so I said, "Let me put it this way, Robyn. There's not enough money in the world to ever make me hurt one of my friends. And you're my friend. You've never given me any grief and you've always been straight with me as far as I know."

She started crying softly and in her voice was a heavy sadness, and relief, too. "I knew you would never hurt me, Kevin. I didn't believe it when I heard it because I always felt we understood each other. I could always be myself with you. I am not surprised by John, however. He's an asshole and his day is coming. He can't control everybody like he used to."

I asked her how Whitney was doing and she sighed. "Well, we're not as tight as we used to be. It's pretty much all business now. I miss her and I have to keep reminding myself she's married now, and pregnant, and that changes a woman." I asked her how the pregnancy was going, and she told me Whitney had developed toxemia, which had caused her blood pressure to rise and her feet and legs to swell.

"She has to stay off her feet most of the time because she's just so *huge*. She must be over two hundred pounds, and her doctor isn't too happy about it. She prays every day, 'Dear God, let this baby be born *now!*' It's really weird seeing her like that, Kevin. She's not my skinny little Nippy anymore."

We talked for a few more minutes and she rang off with, "Please take care of yourself, Kevin. Be very careful from now on. And remember that I love you."

About an hour later, John Houston called me. He was using his extra-nice, hail-fellow-well-met voice. He didn't waste any time getting to the point. "Kevin, did I ever ask you to hurt Robyn Crawford in any way?"

For him to come right out with a question like that, I knew he must have me on the speakerphone and someone was there listening. "What are you trying to do, John? We both know what happened."

He gave a false, hearty laugh and said, "No, no, Kevin. If I did say anything like that, you must have known I was kidding. You sure as hell didn't think I was serious, did you?"

"Yes, John, I *did* think you were serious. In fact, I *know* you were serious. You wouldn't offer me money and a record contract if you were just kidding around."

He went ballistic, screaming and cussing. "You fucking liar! If you ever go public with this shit, I'll flatly deny it and make your life a living hell!" He cussed and carried on some more, screaming, "You won't get away with it, Kevin. I'm warning you, keep your fucking mouth shut or you'll be one sorry bastard!"

He slammed the phone down and I remember thinking, *What a hell of way to start 1993.*

12

A Monster Success

BOBBI KRISTINA HOUSTON BROWN MADE HER DEBUT ON MARCH 4 at the St. Barnabas Medical Center in Livingston, New Jersey. Delivered by cesarean section, she weighed six pounds twelve ounces—not very much, considering the enormous weight Whitney had gained during her pregnancy. The proud daddy was holding his wife's hand when the doctor delivered the baby, and one of the nurses on duty said, "You could see his big smile even behind the surgical mask he was wearing. It lit up his whole face."

When Regina and I heard about the birth of the baby, she broke into tears, sobbing, "I was supposed to be the godmother, now I'll probably never even get to *see* the baby. Damn that fucking dyke, and damn John Houston for getting me fired! I wish they'd both just drop dead!"

Later on that month, John called Regina's attorney, Linda Mensche, and told her if a book was published about the Houston family, Nippy, Inc. would file a lawsuit accusing Ms. Brown and her accomplice, Kevin Ammons, of extortion. Linda laughed and told me they were "unethical scum." She wanted to go forward with the case and file a "wrongful termination" lawsuit against Nippy, Inc., but Regina was hesitant. If it became public that she was an informant to the tabloids, she would be ostracized by the entertainment world. Every celebrity in the business hated the rags and felt nothing but contempt for those who supplied them with personal information.

Regina was soon up to her old tricks again and sold several stories about Oprah Winfrey and Michael Jackson. Since she was no longer privy to information about Whitney and Bobby, she dug up whatever dirt she could on other celebrities. I would often hear her on the phone with Flo Anthony and Jamie Foster Brown, of *Sister 2 Sister*, but if she caught me listening, she would take the phone into the bathroom. Ever since she had been fired in August 1992, she would whine to me this was the only way she could make enough money to meet her overhead.

Several months previously I had lent her five thousand dollars and learned, much to my surprise, she was far from broke. I was spending the day with my sons. When we were in the car, one of the boys said, "Daddy, somebody left a wallet in the backseat." He handed it to me and it wasn't a wallet, it was Regina's savings-account bank book. She had $89,000 in her account. I was livid but kept my cool until I had taken the boys home, then I went to confront Regina.

She said it was an old book, but I had seen the dates. It was current. She started crying, clinging to me, begging me to forgive her, saying she needed the money to pay doctors' bills and "take care of her future" as she was no longer employed. She said, "It's really *our* money, Kevin, because we're in love and we're getting married just as soon as you get a divorce."

She would sob hysterically and threaten to kill herself if I ever left her. She had a little .25 automatic pistol, and on several occasions she had taken it out and pointed it to her head. I was both appalled and fascinated by her.

Five months after the birth of her daughter, Whitney went back on the road. I was dying to see her again so I managed to get tickets to her concert in Miami. The evening was a total disaster. Everybody had to wait outside until just a few minutes before the show started. Then once inside, we had to wait even longer. Concerts never start on schedule, but this one was unusually late. There were two opening acts, and by this time everyone in the audience had become impatient. Finally, at about ten o'clock (an hour and a half past her scheduled curtain time), Whitney strolled onstage, and I could tell by her expression she was in one of her Royal Family snits. She didn't offer a word of apology, just started singing.

At the close of her first number a fan rushed up to the stage and thrust an autograph book at her, begging her to sign. She gave the poor girl a cold, haughty look and said right into the microphone, "Your ticket definitely does say 'seat' on it, doesn't it?"

The audience gasped and erupted in boos and catcalls, but Whitney just tossed her head and growled, "Look, I've been booed before and it really doesn't faze me."

The next day reviewers and disc jockeys blasted her behavior, and call-in shows were filled with disgusted fans who swore they'd never go to another Whitney Houston concert. In a *Miami Herald* review, Leonard Pitts wrote, "Houston took the stage with an attitude that smelled like rotting fish. It was the *Hindenburg* of pop concerts. Her behavior was tacky, unprofessional, arrogant, and beneath the dignity of a singer of her talent and stature."

One of the secretaries at Arista told Regina "the suits" had called Whitney on it and warned her she had better change her prima donna ways or she would get an attitude adjustment. She must have listened because there was no more more bad press during the rest of her tour. In fact, she was more open than she had ever been. She would often bring her baby onstage and introduce her to the audience, then she would call for Bobby to come out and say hello.

Whitney was performing in Monte Carlo on the French Riviera on August 9, 1993, the day she turned thirty years old. Twenty-four-year-old Bobby gave her a birthday party aboard a yacht that was anchored in the Mediterranean—which reminded them both of their honeymoon just a year earlier.

By the end of 1993 *The Bodyguard* had grossed over $400 million worldwide and the sound-track album had sold over 24 million copies, the largest-selling sound track in the history of music. Critics continued to pan Whitney's acting debut even as her fans continued to see the movie three and four times.

"I Will Always Love You" won Number One World Single, Number One Hot Single, and Number One R&B Single at the annual Billboard Music Awards—in all, Whitney picked up eleven awards that night. She also performed at the show, dedicating "I Have Nothing" to her fans and telling them, "There would be no me without you." There were no boos or catcalls this night. The entire audience gave her a three-minute standing ovation.

Regina kept in touch with the staff at Nippy, Inc. and continued to pay for her medical benefits with its Cobra plan so she would pick up bits of gossip from time to time. I was pretty much resigned that I'd never get a record contract. If I couldn't sing for a living, then I wanted to help children. I founded the Power Club, a nonprofit organization in Chicago, and tried to get my life back on track. I was hoping that without the pressures of the Houston family, Regina and I might have a chance together. I should have known better.

In November 1993, I pulled up in front of Regina's building and saw her sitting in a sports car with another man. When she saw me, she jumped out, ran over, and started babbling, "Don't worry, baby, that's just a friend of mine—and he's gay." She was trying to kiss me but I pushed her away and left. This time, I told myself, it was completely over. I didn't return her calls when she paged me, and I tried not to think about her. About a week and a half later I was in my office when I heard over the radio that Whitney Houston's former publicist Regina Brown was engaged to George Daniels, owner of George's Music Room on the west

Whitney at the Grammy Awards in 1994, where she won Best Pop Female Vocalist for "I Will Always Love You" (Moskowitz/Globe)

*(Opposite) "How Will I Know?"
MTV explodes with Whitney
(Mathews/Retna)*

*(Right) Bobby Brown and
Whitney Houston at the Arista
Records pre-Grammy party
(Rose/Globe)*

*(Below) Lovely in concert
(Barrett/Globe)*

(Above) Whitney Houston and Kevin Costner in The Bodyguard *(Rangefinder/Globe)*
(Below) A moment from The Bodyguard *(Rangefinder/Globe)*

(Above) The cast of
Waiting to Exhale:
Whitney Houston, Forest
Whitaker, Angela Basset,
Lela Rochon, and
Loretta Devine
(Rangefinder/Globe)

(Right) In concert in
The Bodyguard
(Rangefinder/Globe)

(Right) Whitney Houston and Denzel Washington on the set of The Preacher's Wife

(Below) On location for the making of The Preacher's Wife, *Whitney's latest film (Davila/Retna)*

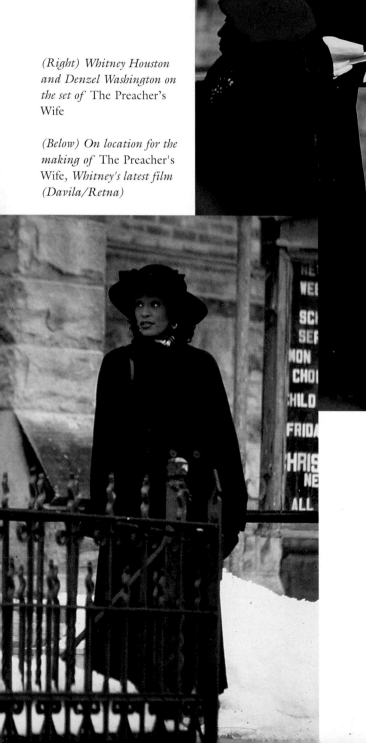

(Above) At the concert for Nelson Mandela in 1988 (Allan/Globe)

(Right) Singing her heart out (Kelly/Globe)

Whitney in concert at Radio City Music Hall (Trupp/Globe)

side. I had introduced them and now they were getting married. It shocked me. I didn't know they had even dated. To hear Regina tell it, I was the only man in her life.

The next time she called, I listened to what she had to say. She swore she was in love with only me but she needed security in her life and knew I would never marry her. She pleaded with me to understand, then said, "I don't want to give you up, baby—I don't want to give up the great sex. I *need* good lovin', so we can just continue seeing each other, can't we? George will never know and nobody will get hurt."

"Sex was all we ever had, anyway," I told her, "so let me know when you need servicing."

Whitney's grueling schedule was beginning to take its toll and she appeared exhausted and even haggard onstage. She was thin and her temper was shorter than usual. Early in 1994 she began a twenty-two-city tour. Tabloids continued to write that her marriage was a sham and she was "closer than ever to her longtime companion, Robyn Crawford." The usually private Crawford was becoming as exasperated by the persistent rumors as Whitney was, and she gave her own interview, stating, "Whitney Houston is a happily married woman, a *traditionally* married woman. She adores her husband and child. The foundation we had years ago, the friendship we shared, is pretty much there in the past.

"Now it's business. Those of us who work for her have to change to accommodate what happens. I would say that, as a person, Whitney has pretty much stayed the same. She is not high-handed or temperamental or arrogant, but although she walks softly, she carries an invisible stick. If you back her up against a wall, you will be sorry. I think it's the people around her, myself included, who have to adjust to the fact that she is now so famous, so in demand."

Unfortunately, fame doesn't always attract just *good* fans. Since 1991, Whitney has been stalked by a deranged drifter, Charles Russell Gilberg, who believes she is his soul mate and that he is the father of Bobbi Kris. He began writing letters promising to be with Whitney and her baby, which understandably terrified her and is just one of the reasons there's such tight security surrounding her family. Early in 1994, Gilberg moved to Newark, New Jersey, to be closer to Whitney, prompting her to obtain a restraining order.

She travels with an entourage of bodyguards, not because she's a prima donna, but because she fears for her life. And she takes her baby with her because she's frightened to let her out of her sight. Fans took her to task for that, too, accusing her of somehow harming the baby by dragging her from city to city, but the fact is that Grandma Cissy is in charge of Bobbi Kris while on the road and gives her all the TLC she could possibly want.

At the twenty-first annual American Music Awards, Whitney won in an impressive eight categories—and, again, at the Grammy Awards, she won Best Pop Female Vocalist for "I Will Always Love You." The sound track for *The Bodyguard* won Album of the Year, and "I Will Always Love You" won Best Record of the Year.

Even though it had started out on such a promising note, 1994 would prove to be a tough year for Whitney. She was not handling well the stress of touring. She was often late for performances, making vague excuses about "throat problems" if she bothered to make excuses at all. Photographers and fans who got too close would be met by a wall of bodyguards and ordered to "Back off!"

Bobby put his career on hold to travel with his wife, and insiders report this put further strain on the marriage. Whitney would call him onstage, leap into his arms, and wrap her legs high up around his body, clinging to him as she told the audience, "I am a woman in love and the man I'm in love with is very much in love with me!" Then she would send him off to the wings where the Royal Family would comment on his sullen embarrassment.

On his twenty-fifth birthday, Whitney threw him a smashing party at the elegant and expensive Tavern on the Green restaurant in New York City. Jamie Foster Brown covered the event for the magazine, *Sister 2 Sister,* and had this to say: "Bobby, his mother, Carole, and Whitney all got onstage to welcome and thank the guests for coming. Bobby's mom was happy. She spoke very emotionally, and disjointedly, and she said she loves all her children. She also said she loves Whitney, not because she's *Whitney Houston* but because she's her daughter-in-law. Bobby said, 'No matter what anybody thinks, my marriage to Whitney is real. And if you don't respect it, then fuck all of you!' "

After the party in the pressroom, a physical confrontation broke out between Bobby and a photographer who had been hired to cover the party. Reportedly, the photographer made a comment about Bobby's mother that the hotheaded bad boy didn't appreciate, so he backhanded him across the face. Those close to the couple say the tension of touring with his wife was making him increasingly testy and sullen. Whitney can be demanding, and Bobby wasn't used to being relegated to the position of "he's with Whitney"—his earlier fears of becoming Mr. Whitney Houston seemed to be coming true and it tweaked his ego.

Whitney wearily told one reporter, "How famous can you be? How many number one songs can you have? Having all these things, having money and all that, didn't make me happy. And nobody understands that. It's always, 'Oh, girl, to be in your shoes!' but they have no idea. They are clueless!"

The Bodyguard had become such an enormous hit that by the spring of 1994 movie studios were deluging Whitney with scripts. The only one she showed any interest in was *The Bishop's Wife,* a remake of the 1940s tearjerker starring Carry Grant, Loretta Young, and David Niven. But she had a concert tour to complete so, as in the case of *The Bodyguard,* she told the studio she would get back to them when she was free of her obligations.

Tensions between Bobby and Robyn finally erupted in March. The Royal Family was staying at the Peninsula Hotel in Beverly Hills, and Whitney and Bobby had been observed on several occasions arguing publicly between themselves and with Robyn. As reported in Jeffrey Bowman's *Diva,* security guards were summoned early on the morning of March 24 by Robyn Crawford: "When we arrived at the hotel room, Robyn Crawford answered the door. She had a scratch on her hand and red marks on her arms and neck. Although she played down any incident that may have happened, something was clearly wrong. After a few moments, Whitney Houston's own security personnel, who had apparently also been summoned, arrived.

"Mr. Brown was cursing and threatening Ms. Crawford and we asked Ms. Houston if she would like us to stay until the police, who had also been summoned, arrived. But she said she could handle the situation from here. We noticed by his behavior that Mr. Brown had apparently been drinking. It seemed that Brown, Houston, and Crawford had all been involved in some sort of physical altercation."

For the next couple of months both the legitimate press and the tabloids reported on the numerous public arguments between the battling Browns. They didn't seem to mind who was around when they got into one of their high-voltage spats. Bobby's money woes were mounting, his career was in the dumper, and his wife just kept getting more popular and richer. She appeared on the *Forbes* magazine list of the world's top-earning entertainers at number twenty-three, with an income of $33 million.

"Bobby's self-esteem took a nosedive," a friend of Regina's told us. "He was served with a writ from the IRS for over three million dollars in back taxes, and he didn't have it and had no way of getting it. Whitney had bailed him out before, but now that they're fighting all the time, he doesn't think she will be there for him again."

Insiders say the constant bickering wasn't over money but women. On more than one occasion, Bobby was seen with females who were clearly not his wife. But it seemed no matter how much Whitney might fight with her husband about these issues, when confronted by a reporter, she staunchly stood by her man. She told *Ebony* magazine, "Marriage is a beautiful institution. People don't know Bobby because there hasn't been that much on Bobby except that Bobby is this sexy many who does all this bumping and grinding. But Bobby is a family man. Bobby loves his mother, loves his family. He goes out when he wants to hear music, when he wants to know what's happening. He comes home. I know where my husband is; I know what my husband does. There are certain things I don't go for and Bobby knows that. And there's stuff he doesn't go for. That's why we can be together, because we both have the same standards."

She went on to say she had heard the rumors that "two successful black people cannot make it as a couple. Is this why black women sometimes marry white men? Bobby and I work it out because we are determined to make it work. And it works because we trust each other and we don't trust what people tell us. Bobby and I are man and woman. We're married, we have a kid, we go through things, we have our fights like everybody else."

Bobby continued to tour with Whitney even though the tabloids had them breaking up and reconciling on a weekly basis. Then in June, Whitney called Bobby onstage as she often did at the beginning of her performance and told him the joyous news that she was pregnant again. The audience screamed their approval while the Browns kissed passionately.

"I've never found anything in life more fulfilling than being a mother," Whitney said, beaming. "I can't wait to have a little brother or sister for Bobbi Kris. We'd like to have three kids, and I hope this one will be a boy."

But it wasn't meant to be. She had a miscarriage a month later.

After less than a week's rest, she was back on the concert circuit with Bobby by her side. Fans said she seemed drawn and haggard and her temper was even shorter than usual. Her tardiness to performances continued and she had a "go to hell" attitude if anyone dared call her on it. In August, while appearing in Anaheim, California, she stunned the audience by tearfully asking that the spotlight be turned on the children of O. J. Simpson and Nicole Brown, Sydney and Justin, who were in the audience. Tears ran down her cheeks and she seemed unaware of the shocked gasps from the audience. Said one fan, "It was mortifying and very weird—everyone was embarrassed."

Another added, "Sydney and Justin looked really uncomfortable and I thought it was in bad taste to do that to those poor kids. Haven't they had enough spotlights on them to last a lifetime?"

Personally, 1994 had been a year from hell for Whitney, but professionally she had racked up a staggering number of awards and adulations. That fall she and her entourage flew to South Africa for a three-week engagement in what was called "the biggest media event since the inauguration of Nelson Mandela." Whitney's show brought together music, liberation, history, and love as more than seventy thousand black, white, and brown South Africans packed Johannesburg's Ellis Park Stadium. It was the first time any concert had brought together South Africans of all races and political parties and temporarily linked South Africa and the United States via an HBO hookup, which carried the event to millions of viewers.

Billed simply "Whitney—the Concert for a New South Africa"—she had entered the exclusive club of one-name global superstars. Dressed in a stunning gold gown that clung to her slender figure, she walked onstage waving U.S. and South African flags in both hands. The gown was accented with bold African designs of a breastplate with long dangling beads and large gold medallions that fell to below her crotch. Shoulder-length, brightly beaded earrings set off her gold turban, which was held together at the center of her forehead with a jeweled clasp.

The one touchy moment in an otherwise smashing tour was when she referred to the controversial Winnie Mandela as "your queen" and was met by a barrage of boos from the audience. Ever feisty, Whitney tossed her head and retorted, "I don't care what you think!"

The rest of the three-week engagement went smoothly as Whitney wowed them in Durban and Cape Town, toured

Soweto, and visited several orphanages. Newspaper headlines announced, "The Queen of Pop Visits King Mswati III," in Swaziland. She told reporters she was "most impressed by the pride, the strength, and the dignity of the people in the face of what appears to be insurmountable odds. This feels like my spiritual home and I'd love the opportunity to return for another visit."

She graciously submitted to several photo sessions with President Mandela and at one point wept openly on his shoulder. Cissy, who had accompanied her daughter, was invited onstage in Cape Town and gave a rousing performance of one of her old gospel tunes. Bobbi Kris stayed in the States with a nanny.

Back in the States fans and reporters were still sniping at both Whitney and Bobby. Stories of drug use and drug deals continued to follow Bobby wherever he went—and he continued to answer the charges with his fists. When Whitney wasn't fighting *with* him, she was fighting *for* him, constantly reassuring fans (and herself) that her marriage was a good one. Rumors surfaced in late 1994 that he'd gotten another woman pregnant, and it was finally confirmed that he'd fathered a fourth child, born just after his marriage in 1992. He is currently facing a paternity suit in that case.

Every movie magazine that carried a story on Whitney also carried letters from disgruntled fans who had become fed up with the most unlikely duo of the decade. Everyone, it seemed, was tired of the public bickering and reports of more discord between the battling Browns. One such letter, written to *Fresh!* magazine, summed up the general feeling among fans:

"Whitney Houston spends all of her time trying to convince people how wonderful her dumb husband is and gets upset because people say she's married to the wrong kind of person. What did she expect? She used to be so nice and good, and he spends half his time getting someone pregnant and then dumps them. The only reason he didn't dump her is because she's rich and can do a lot for his career."

That seemed to be the opinion of almost every reporter who interviewed the couple, and they questioned the logic of such a union. "If you can't get along, get a divorce, but please spare us the constant washing of your dirty linen in public."

Pamela Howell, a freelance writer for *Atlanta*, had a very interesting experience with Bobby Brown. She went backstage to interview him after a local awards show and hadn't spoken more than a few words before "he started hugging and kissing me. He had me in a headlock at one point. He never answered any of my questions. He just wanted to grope me. He acted like a thug."

While Bobby's prickly, street-tough persona raised the hackles of fans and reporters, Whitney's innate *likability* kept her popularity high. She was tough and humble, soft and hard as nails, possessing gratitude *and* attitude. She could swear like a longshoreman one moment then praise God the next. Her face could take on the curled-lip sneer of arrogance if someone displeased her, then soften into a glowing Madonna when gazing into the face of her child. She was a paradox, and that's what kept the public interested in her every move.

She told *Ebony* magazine, "My mother sang with me in her stomach; I sang with Bobbi Kris in my stomach. I believe the child starts to develop within, and whatever is put inside you, whatever you read, whatever you think, whatever you do, affects the child. So basically I just read and listened to music. And I traveled with my husband on the road, so Bobbi Kris heard music constantly."

"Whitney is a normal person who likes to do normal things and would like to lead a normal life," Cissy said. "But of course, she can't."

13

Three Thumbs Up

WHITNEY CLOSED OUT 1994 WITH A MUCH NEEDED REST AT HER estate in New Jersey and started reading the pile of scripts that had been accumulating since the release of *The Bodyguard*. She had read the script for *The Bishop's Wife* several months ago and thought it would be fun to try her hand at comedy. The darkness and drama of *The Bodyguard* had emotionally drained her as the story line was so similar to her own life: international singing superstar stalked by deranged fan.

(In May 1994, Whitney got her second restraining order, against another overly zealous fan. Part-time carpenter Steve Marriott besieged her with dozens of flowers, love notes, and phone calls. When police investigated, they found a cache of weapons including a crossbow and several rifles and knives. He served two months and was released.)

Then Whitney received a phone call from Terry McMillan, author of the wildly successful novel *Waiting to Exhale*. Her book was to be made into a movie, and she wanted Whitney for the part of the lead character, Savannah. Not only had black women fallen in love with the four sassy, outspoken, zany girlfriends, but so had every other woman.

Briefly, the story is about four close female friends who have nothing but trouble with the men in their lives. They keep finding a lot of the wrong men when all they want is one good man who will live up to the standards each woman has set for herself. They band together, ever optimistic they'll find their soul mate. Poignant, gritty, and realistic, the book also has some wonderful moments of levity.

This story appealed to Whitney because she would be part of an ensemble, rather than carrying the picture as the only female lead. She needed a break from touring as life on the road was lived at such a high-energy, frenetic pace it exhausted her. The slow pace of movie making would give her a chance to catch her breath.

Shooting started on *Waiting to Exhale* in the spring of 1995 with the talented actor-director Forest Whitaker directing. The location was sunny, peaceful Scottsdale, Arizona, which helped Whitney relax and concentrate on acting.

Terry McMillan said, "She's going to be a really better actress when she starts seeing herself as an actress and not a singer who acts."

Angela Bassett had the showiest role, that of Bernadine, whose adulterous husband leaves her for his white secretary after twelve years of marriage. She gets revenge by stuffing his belongings into his expensive sports car and setting them on fire. Lela Rochon is Robin, a successful businesswoman who keeps falling for no-good pretty boys who break her heart, and Loretta Devine plays Gloria, who turns to food for comfort when she finds out her ex-husband is gay. Whitney's role is also that of a professional businesswoman, but unlike party girl Robin, Savannah clings to a doomed relationship with a married man who strings her along.

While on location in Arizona, Whitney told *Ebony* magazine, "In just two weeks, Forest has taught me a lot about acting. In

The Bodyguard I was just simply playing a character that I was familiar with because she and I had the same kind of world. With Savannah, it's more like me without the fame. She allows me to be a lot more like myself. The great thing about it is that I have three other beautiful ladies who are all great actresses and whom I can play off of."

Terry McMillan said, "Everybody is trying to find out if Whitney is a bitch. She isn't. She's really down. She's blacker than most people think. I like her."

Keeping the movie "black" was important to McMillan, and she insisted on a black director as well as black women in important positions and a black crew (over 65 percent of the film crew was African-American).

Most days the quartet of actresses rose at six in the morning and often worked late into the night. Whitney appreciated the loving support she got on the set and remembers confessing her nervousness to Angela Bassett, who told her to "just go in there and just do it." Working with Forest was also a great experience, and she credits him with making her look so good. "Forest cares right down to the last detail. He's very focused and makes you feel very comfortable, like working with your brother. He asked me not to take acting lessons but just be natural, be myself. He is a dear friend."

Exhale is being acclaimed as a breakthrough film because it portrays black women as not only caring mothers but strong, professional, successful women as well. Some critics charged that it was too rough on black men, presenting them as either heartless womanizers or pathetic losers, but Whitney defends the characters. "How come men can tell stories about women the way they want to tell them, and then when women tell stories, it's male-bashing?"

McMillan told *Ebony,* "I hope people will understand that black women love and care for black men . . . they are not always jealous and envious of each other. We are really supportive and have a sense of sisterhood, at least intelligent women do. We all want to be loved and appreciated, without being taken advantage of. We want to know that somebody's got our back, because we want them [black men] to know we've got theirs."

The talented supporting cast of men included Gregory Hines, Bill Cobbs, Dennis Haysbert, Wendell Pierce, and Leon Kelly Preston.

Even as Whitney was defending the male characters in the movie, her own strong black man was getting into his usual scraps. He threw a party in West Hollywood in August, and when a security guard told him to keep the noise down, he kicked him!

Bad boy Bobby also faced charges of aggravated battery and disorderly conduct for an altercation along with three of his "boys" at Walt Disney World's Mannequins nightclub in Orlando, Florida. When a Chicago businessman approached a woman the trio had been talking to, they jumped him, hit him over the head with a bottle, and beat him to the floor. When the police arrived, they ordered the four young men to sit on the curb while they talked to witnesses, but Bobby refused. "It had to do with his clothes," said Jim Solomons, a spokesman for the Orange County Sheriff's Office. "He didn't want to get them dirty."

When he was placed in the squad car, Bobby urinated in the backseat, then carved obscenities into the seat cover with his pen. The victim was taken to a local hospital where he underwent emergency surgery to reattach his nearly severed ear. Bobby and his boys spent less than five hours in jail and were released on $5,000 bail. (He was arraigned on a misdemeanor assault charge, December 29, 1995.) Whitney, who was on tour in Asia, had no comment.

Bobby was almost killed in late September when his bodyguard Steven "Shot" Sealy was shot to death while sitting in the passenger seat of Brown's car, a cream-colored, $295,000 Bentley, registered in Whitney's name. Sealy, who had just started working for Bobby after serving a two-year sentence on weapons charges, was also engaged to Bobby's kid sister, Carol. Bobby and Sealy were leaving a bar in Roxbury in Boston when a fusillade of bullets cracked store windows and peppered the sidewalk, killing Sealy. "They shot my boy!" Bobby yelled.

During that month he was seen hitting all the nightspots, telling friends he had left Whitney and showing them his empty ring finger. Whitney shrugged it off, telling *Time* magazine she knew her marriage was rocky but said the media exaggerated her marital woes. "I could tell you about some fouled-up marriages, but it ain't my business. They want to mess with us all the time. I married the brother I want to be with, and they [the media] didn't understand it or like it, so therefore they tried to fuck with me; white America tried to fuck with me. They thought, 'Hard boy, good girl'—it doesn't work."

When Bobby visited his wife on location in Arizona, they were often seen walking arm in arm, laughing and snuggling together like newlyweds. Lela Rochon said, "I got the feeling that she loved her husband. Even when he had trouble in Orlando, it was never a threat of them splitting up."

"His behavior may be extreme," Jamie Foster Brown has said, "but I feel it's a cry for help. People forget that when he met Whitney he was a big star in his own right, with three platinum records and a veritable sex-symbol status. He put his career on hold to travel with her, and that has to have caused problems in the marriage. Bobby has a lot of pride and ego, and to be shoved aside by people trying to get to his wife has to hurt."

With his career in trouble and his personal life out of control, Bobby continued to act up in public, causing reporters to pose that same old question: "Why does she put up with it? Why does she stay with him when she could have any man she wanted?"

"Because I love my sexy baby," Whitney says. "This has got to be worth fighting for."

She told a concert crowd in Vienna, Virginia, "My husband and I and the baby are very happy. You heard it from the horse's mouth. Don't believe what you hear and what you read."

Inadvertently, I was the cause of more controversy for Whitney. On March 13, 1995, I filed a lawsuit claiming defamation of character against Regina. She had made my life a living hell for the past three years and I wanted revenge. She continued to blame me for her current woes, telling me if only I had taken John Houston up on his offer, I would be under contract and making my own records. She wanted to get even with John for firing her, but she was too frightened to do it directly. "You have no idea how powerful and ruthless that man is," she told me. So she got to him through me.

After I filed my lawsuit, a story appeared in one of the tabloids claiming, "Whitney Houston's bodyguard real-life hit man!" The article went on to tell how I had been contacted by the superstar's own father to "rough up" her lesbian lover, Robyn Crawford. My phone started ringing and didn't stop for the next two weeks as the media descended on me like vultures. Everybody wanted to interview the "hit man," and I was courted by every entertainment magazine in the country. The *National Enquirer, Star,* and the *Globe* all ran stories on me, and I appeared on the TV show *American Journal* to "tell my side" and to set the record straight.

After the show aired, Robyn called and told me I shouldn't be talking to the media. "It will just open up another can of peas. We all need to keep a low profile."

For the next two weeks I received nightly calls, usually between two and three in the morning, with someone warning me to "keep your fucking mouth shut about the Houstons or you're going to end up very dead!" It was terrifying to be awakened from a sound sleep to hear someone threatening to kill me or break my arms and legs. I admit I became a little paranoid and started carrying a pistol with me wherever I went. I was sorry about bringing more attention to Whitney even though I wasn't the one who went to the press with the story. Regina was interviewed and stated that she had been there when the conversation between John and me took place; she heard everything.

I was still in touch with Whitney's brother, Michael, and I would often get together with him for a night on the town. He and his stepbrother, Gary, had been in and out of a dozen rehab centers, but every time I saw them, they were still doing drugs.

Michael was staying at the Hotel Sofitel in Chicago one weekend and invited me over to smoke some weed with him. He told me his father had finally admitted that he had treated me wrong and that he had "to make it right by Kevin. As soon as everything blows over, I'll give him a call and we'll get his music career rollin'."

"Yeah, right!" I said to Michael. "How many times have I heard that before?"

"Probably as many times as I have," he answered. I knew Michael wanted a singing career as badly as I did, and I knew he had been given false hope and empty promises by John just as I had. He had a good voice, and often when we would get together, we would sing all the old tunes we both grew up with. I knew he was hurt and bitter that his sister wouldn't help him out, and I knew that was the reason he was stoned most of the time.

As we sat passing a joint between us, I asked how the marriage was working out and he snorted, "Huh! I had to knock Bobby on his ass the other day. He slapped Nippy, so I popped him one—knocked his ass out cold."

While Bobby continued to rack up lawsuits, Whitney was in the studio recording the sound track for *Waiting to Exhale,* which was being produced by Kenneth "Babyface" Edmonds. She wanted the album to feature only women and gathered a virtual who's who of R&B legends—Aretha Franklin, Toni Braxton, Chaka Kahn, and Mary J. Blige—to join her on the sound track.

Whitney was pleased with her performance in *Exhale* and was anxious to get to work on her next film project, *The Bishop's Wife,* which had been rewritten and retitled *The Preacher's Wife.* It's a charming Christmas love story about an angel (Denzel Washington) who comes down from heaven to help a preacher (Courtney Vance) build a church. The preacher's neglected wife (Whitney) is attracted to him, much to her chagrin, but it gives rise to a merry mix-up. The 1947 classic featured Cary Grant as the angel, David Niven as the preacher, and Loretta Young in the role Whitney would reprise.

Shooting wouldn't start until early January 1996, so it gave Whitney time to work on her troubled marriage. Close friends were saying the couple faced an uncertain future, but Whitney took to the airwaves to deny it, telling Barbara Walters, "I want this marriage to be a success, to last until the end of time—whenever that is." She admitted it was difficult at times, balancing a thriving career in both music and films with marriage and motherhood. Especially with her high-profile lifestyle and the public's insatiable interest in her every move. Reporters hung out in bars they knew Bobby frequented to see whom he would show up with and if he was wearing his wedding band.

In September 1995, Bobby appeared at New York's trendy China Club with Dennis Rodman, Rodman's girlfriend, and another beautiful woman in tow. They partied until dawn with Bobby acting more like a bachelor than a married man. And just to make sure no one missed it, he held up his ringless left hand. The tabloids couldn't keep up with the on-again, off-again battling Browns as every week brought more speculation and more publicity. They appeared together in New York on September 14 for the T. J. Martel Foundation Humanitarian Award ceremony honoring Clive Davis, then a week later Bobby was seen partying it up, sans ring.

A family member told me, "Bobby's having one hell of a time dealing with it, the relentless media attention, the fact that his wife is a global superstar. He's rebelling against the control she has over him, financial and otherwise. With old John 'managing' her and Cissy 'advising' her, Bobby doesn't stand a chance. And doing drugs just magnifies the situation. The only way he's gonna get his career back on track is to put down the dope."

Whitney continued to fight for her rocky marriage. Bobbi Kris was two years old and Whitney didn't want to be a single mother. In fact, she wanted another baby and told *Redbook*, "Kids have a way of bringing purity back to life. That's what's important. To raise children. Decent human beings. To keep my husband happy. Old-fashioned stuff, but through all the madness and the peaks and the cool-downs, I've maintained my basic values."

Basic family values had always been important to Bobby before he had been sidetracked. Sadly, it took the shooting death of his friend and bodyguard Shot Sealy and the threat of losing his family to get his attention. In October and November of 1995, he underwent treatment for alcohol addiction at the Betty Ford Clinic in Rancho Mirage, California, and also at the Charter Peachford Hospital in Atlanta, Georgia. TV's nightly news showed a nervous Bobby pacing the parking lot outside the Betty Ford Clinic, chain-smoking and stalling for time. He was clearly having second thoughts and was reluctant to take that final step. A few days after his release, he was seen drinking and partying with a bare ring finger.

November 7, the *Globe* carried a story headlined, " 'Whitney Cheated on Me With Gals!' Shattered Bobby Brown confesses all in drug rehab." Bobby reportedly said, "I was unfaithful and abused her when I was high. I drank forty-eight bottles of beer and five glasses of brandy a day. I'm heartbroken and feel like half a man. Whitney made me feel so low, like I was nothing, every time she went off with a woman."

Whitney and Bobby were very publicly together again on November 17 at Bar None, a Miami hot spot owned by director Oliver Stone. Led by the beaming Browns, the entourage swept into the VIP room and ordered several bottles of Cristal champagne. "The bottle's out of my life for good now," Bobby told a *Time* magazine reporter, but he drank two beers. Whitney was stunning in a slinky black dress that showed off her model-thin figure, and Bobby was on his best behavior. This time it was Whitney who got a little pushy with a fan. A young woman approached Bobby and asked for his autograph. Bobby politely declined, but Whitney wasn't so gracious. Clearly irritated, she turned on the startled fan and snapped, "*Please* leave him alone!"

Less than two weeks later, Bobby was spotted in New York City at the birthday party for hip-hop impresario Sean "Puffy" Combs. Witnesses say he was making out all night with a pretty but unidentified young woman. And there was no shortage of booze.

Whitney chose to ignore the rumors flying around her and took a much-needed breather. The premiere of *Waiting to Exhale* was due December 22, and it was the holidays and she wouldn't let anything upset Bobbi Kris's third Christmas.

On December 2, at a benefit honoring her achievements in films and music, held at New York's City Center, Whitney arrived conspicuously single. She was regal from head to toe, again wearing all black, which caused some people to speculate that she was in mourning for her lost marriage. Tears filled her eyes as she accepted her award, and she smiled down at her daughter, who was sitting in the front row. "You are my reason for being," she said softly. She did not mention her husband's name.

Bobby was also in New York City that night and was seen hitting several hot, trendy clubs and partying with a variety of different women. Again he was not wearing his ring.

The sound track of *Waiting to Exhale* was released early in December and immediately began selling out. Of Whitney's three solos, two became hits, "Shoop-Shoop" and "Why Does It Hurt So Bad?" But she wasn't resting on her laurels, she was at work on a gospel sound track for *The Preacher's Wife* and also scouting around for new projects. She signed a development deal with Disney Studios and purchased the rights to Dorothy Dandridge's life story.

Whitney told *Time* magazine, "I heard Janet Jackson wanted to play Dorothy very badly. If I feel it in my soul, I'll do it. If not, maybe I'll let Janet do it."

She planned to record a greatest-hits album and she told *Ebony* she definitely wanted another child. "One more, and I'm praying it'll be a son." She admitted she was still fighting to keep her family together. "This is a stressful life. It takes a lot of time and energy. I don't want to be doing this like when I'm old. I want to be sitting back, watching my kids and grandkids."

She spent the holidays with Bobby (when he wasn't out on the town) and Bobbi Kris (the two B's, she calls them), catching up with friends by phone and reading scripts. She and her father were working together to develop a remake of the classic tearjerker *A Star Is Born*—Whitney Houston style.

She said, "My hope for Bobbi Kris is for her to always be true to herself, no matter what people might say or think. You have to do what you think is right—what you know is right. Be true to yourself. Be a decent human being. I don't have dreams like I want her to become a singer or a doctor or a lawyer. I want my daughter to be a good human being and a God-fearing child. Then everything else will fall into place."

Bobby admitted that he and Whitney were no longer living together. "We've fought a lot," he said, "but it's never gone this far. I'm hoping that when I get sober, we can pick up where we left off and salvage this relationship. I miss my daughter. I want her to have a daddy who's there for her."

While promoting *Waiting to Exhale,* Whitney was asked by a reporter, "Will you ever get married again?"

"Married *again*? I *am* married!" She shook her hand with the enormous ten-carat diamond ring and gold band. "See? It's true Bobby and I are having some problems, but we'll work them out."

On November 27, she and her three costars appeared on *Oprah* to plug their movie, and Oprah Winfrey was told, "Ms. Houston won't discuss her private life." At times Whitney looked tired and sad; other times she appeared belligerent, even sullen. When Oprah asked if her life paralleled in any way that of the troubled, lovelorn character she portrayed in the movie, she snapped, "That's none of your business!" Oprah was shocked speechless and Whitney added softly, "Bobby is fine. That's all I want to say." She ducked her head as tears came to her eyes and reached quickly for her hand-kerchief, and Angela Bassett took her hand, comforting her.

"We've got an hour," Oprah said gently. "Do you want to talk about it?"

Whitney shook her head no and pulled herself together for the next segment.

She was under a great deal of stress and leaned heavily on her parents and Robyn for support. At a party Arista Records gave her for her new CD, everybody was already whispering about Bobby before she arrived. She swept into New York's Equitable Building surrounded by her usual entourage and flanked on all sides by her mother, father, and Robyn. She told reporters she was going to stick by her husband while he went through rehab before making any important decisions on her marriage. She still felt it was worth saving.

Whitney's publicist, Lois Smith, said it was Bobby's idea to enter rehab, that Whitney had not threatened to leave him, as the press had reported. "They both want this marriage to work. Bobby had something to prove, don't you think? I think she's at the end of her rope, but everyone hates to see a marriage end and she's going to wait and see what he does."

"I've got a good man," Whitney says. "We can make it work."

Bobby completed his six weeks of treatment at the Betty Ford Clinic without further incident. In *Time* magazine, December 4, 1995, he says, "I'm definitely fit and over that [alcohol and drugs] hump. I've been in the business a long time and the pressure wears on you. I went to that old bottle. The bottle's out of my life now, so everything is all good. Whitney and I are courting right now. It keeps it exciting. We love each other so dearly, so it's not hard for us to step away from each other a little while because we do love each other."

Whitney liked the new and improved Bobby and told *Ebony* he was very romantic, "just like he used to be before the wedding. He sends me flowers and beautiful cards and leaves little love notes on my pillow. He opens doors, pulls out my chair for me, and treats me like a queen. I'd be crazy to throw this brother away!"

This was a peaceful period for Whitney, who was happier than she had ever been. People would see her tooling around in her white Porsche (or Jeep or lavender limousine), "and she always beeps her horn and waves," said a waiter who worked catered affairs for both her bridal shower and her wedding supper. "She's very friendly and down-to-earth. The night of her shower, she came into the kitchen and signed autographs for everybody. Yes, she let me take her picture."

Everyone involved in the making of *Waiting to Exhale* were sure it would be a hit, but none of them were prepared for the gigantic blockbuster it would become. In theaters all over the country, the cheering, stomping, and applauding was so loud it drowned out the sound track of the movie. Black women spoke about the movie as if testifying in church: "It was a spiritual experience—like watching your own life or those of women you know."

On December 29, 1995, an article in the *Seattle Gay News* said: *Waiting to Exhale* should garner Oscar nominations for Bassett, who finally hits her high mark, and Houston, who shines brilliantly. For director Whitaker, an Oscar should be the least of his due praise; the most important will come from appreciative black women, who will see themselves and know they are beautiful, strong, and capable creatures."

Movie reviewers gushed: "*Exhale* is in a class by itself. This film takes an unflinching look at the lives of four extraordinary black women who share successes and losses while searching for that elusive dream of perfect love."

Filmplex (an entertainment page on the Internet) by Kastle:

She is one of the greatest divas of the music world . . . but Whitney Houston won't stop there. Her debut film and sound track, *The Bodyguard,* became a phenomenal bestseller, cementing her status as hottest new chanteuse of the nineties. While her problem-riddled marriage to singer Bobby Brown and her snide attitude toward the media make her unpopular tabloid fodder, it isn't slowing down her ambition or success one bit.

The proof is in Houston's return to film in *Waiting to Exhale,* as one of four women trying to find love and happiness in an emotionally dysfunctional world. Houston brings depth and poignancy to her role as Savannah, proving her talent as an actress. Her beauty and charisma set the screen on fire. Along with her starring role, she also recorded three songs and produced the film's sound track with studio mastermind Babyface.

Wating to Exhale gives us strong characters and believable situations that are at once culturally particular and universally applicable. Women of every race will fall in love with these sassy black women and see themselves in every tear and broken promise. Angela Bassett and Whitney Houston are Oscar shoo-ins for their stunning portrayals.

Siskel and Ebert gave the movie two thumbs up, and before the month was over, women across the country were holding "Shoop Shoop" parties. After viewing the movie for the fourth or fifth time, they would gather at someone's home, play the sound track, drink a little wine, and discuss and rehash the relationships of the four women. Men's groups and some critics claimed the movie bashed men, and it was compared to *The Color Purple,* which had indeed shown black men to be chauvinistic bullies and insensitive boors.

Whitney defended the movie, saying, "I'd like people to leave the theater knowing that they have been schooled, let in on something that they maybe didn't know much about before. I hope they will enjoy watching the film as much as I enjoyed making it."

Angela Bassett said, "It was a sisterhood immediately. The four of us bonded. Whitney is a very special lady. I felt blessed to meet her and work with her and come to know her. Lela Rochon and Loretta Devine were perfectly cast in their supporting roles. Forest brings together some incredible talent. These are all immensely talented performers. To see them all in one film, you will be blown away. You will just fall in love with all the women—and the men, too."

Wesley Snipes, who also appears in the movie, asked that he not be billed in the credits. He didn't want his fans to think *Exhale* was another Wesley Snipes action flick.

Bassett went on to say, "They [the moviegoing audience] will get some insights into relationships as friends and insights into relationships as lovers. We all want someone to love us. We need friends to sustain us, and we need lovers to shore us up. Sometimes it works and sometimes it doesn't. Friendship, whether platonic or romantic, is the foundation. And we forget that sometimes in our rush to be intimate and close."

Critics claimed Whitney was perfectly typecast as a strong, successful, yet troubled woman in love with the wrong man. "Tough-as-nails Houston plays her character with such cool detachment it is often jarring. Her icy beauty is riveting," wrote a *Filmplex* reviewer.

Obvious comparisons to her own rocky relationship were made, and Whitney said, for perhaps the hundredth time, "My husband is a *good* man. He might not be perfect, but he loves me. Then they try to fix him. Bobbi Kristina is our jewel, our reason for being. She is my whole life now. I never thought I could love as much as I love her. I never thought I could worry so much, and she's only two years old. She teaches me more about love every day."

Bobby's brother, Tommy, said, "He's trying to get his life back together, which includes winning his battle with the bottle and getting his career back on track. This is a hard gig for him after the lifestyle he's led. The music scene is rough and Bobby grew up in it. He was just a teenager when he started singing with the band New Edition, a hotheaded, pugnacious street kid who'd been smoking pot and drinking beer since he was twelve. Then suddenly he was thrown into the limelight and earning more money than he'd ever dreamed possible. He was famous. Everywhere he went, people knew his name. It went to his head."

Watching him gyrate sensually onstage, groping his crotch and simulating sexual intercourse with thrusting hips, women of all ages went crazy. Groupies mobbed him after each performance, and the lucky ones pulled him into the nearest hotel room, begging him to make love to them. He was too much of a gentleman to refuse. He was also a teenager whose libido was tap-dancing on his hormones. It was like being in a big candy store and being told to take your pick.

True to the old saying "The difference between men and boys is the price of their toys," Bobby was soon replacing beer with expensive cognac and fine champagne. He could now afford the very best marijuana, all plump buds, no more street shake for this kid. He traveled with his "homeboys," who looked like inner-city gang members with their baggy pants, baseball caps turned backward, heavy, lethal-looking gold rings on all their fingers, and an attitude nobody wanted to mess with. A couple of them even had a front tooth crowned in pure gold, giving them an ominous leer. Bobby took them everywhere he went and treated them to all-night parties at the most exclusive nightspots in town. They were more than welcome to the leftover groupies, and the good times continued to roll.

Bobby was just twenty-two when he met Whitney, and he still had some wild oats to sow. Then almost thirty, she was ready to settle down. Bobby admits that he fell in love with her the first time he laid eyes on her at an awards show and knew he would marry her someday. He just didn't realize that day would come so soon or that it would change his life forever.

"Bobby is a good kid with a good heart," his brother said, "but the pressures of being Mr. Whitney Houston eventually became too much for him. He was often shunted aside by fans clamoring to get to Whitney."

Friends say Bobby did some real soul-searching in the fall of 1995. He missed and loved his wife and daughter and wanted to go home. Drugs and booze were not a panacea for his inner turmoil, and they didn't give him the solace they once had. He admits it was the hardest thing he'd ever done, all by himself, walking through the door of the Betty Ford Clinic, but "it saved my life," he says. "And it saved my marriage."

14

The Highest-Paid
Black Actress

WHILE SHOOTING *WAITING TO EXHALE* AND WORKING ON THE
sound track with Forest Whitaker, Whitney made it clear she did
not want to sing on the album. "I just wanted to concentrate on
my acting because I'm playing on-screen with Angela Bassett, and
I'm thinking, 'God, if you don't learn nothing from this girl, you
just don't learn nothing at all.' " She wanted the album to showcase the talents of some of her favorite singers, a sort of cross-
generational affair with newcomers such as Brandy and Mary J.
Blige getting down with old pros Aretha Franklin, Patti LaBelle,
TLC, and Chaka Khan. Soul sisters Chanté Moore and Sonja
Marie also appear on the diva-driven album.

Whitaker hired R&B's Babyface to write both a song and the
instrumental score for the movie, and he wanted Whitney to sing
a couple of his new tunes. "Face," as Whitney calls him, was an
old friend from way back, and together they had come up with

the idea of mirroring the movie's female bonding by having only females sing on the track.

"I'm tired of sound tracks where you slap a bunch of artists together and have a hit," Babyface said. "I wanted for it all to make sense." As the movie was being shot, he would visit the set and pick out singers who best brought out the scene's subtext. "I wanted to make sure it wasn't too urban, because the women's stories were wider than that."

Whitney has three solos on the album, "Count on Me," "Exhale (Shoop Shoop)," and "Why Does It Hurt So Bad?" where her pop sensibility serves as a point of stylistic departure in the otherwise R&B-flavored songfest. "Sort of a rap-meets-rhapsody," Babyface said. He was right on target, blending Whitney's pleasant, soft-edged commerciality with the sexually explicit, cutting-edge hip-hop and the funky-lush blues. He had written "Why Does It Hurt So Bad?" for Whitney two years ago, but she had turned it down.

"I wasn't really in the mood for singing about why it hurts so bad," Whitney said. She had been married a few months at the time and was still a happy newlywed, but two years later, the emotions of the movie merged with the real-life circumstances of her troubled relationship with Bobby. "As life would have it," Whitney says, "I'm now ready to sing not only of the joys of things, but the pain of things, too."

She didn't have to sing at all and wouldn't have if not for Babyface's input into the album. "She didn't have to," Whitaker said. "She was hired for a nonsinging role. I would've been happy for her just to act. It [the decision to sing] kind of organically came about."

When the album debuted, Whitney's single "Exhale (Shoop Shoop)" went straight to the top. It was the first time a single had ever entered the pop charts in any of the top five positions in its first week of release. After a string of wheezy fall releases, the nation's music retailers could use a couple of surefire Whitney Houston hits, and they had it with the *Exhale* sound track.

The sixteen-song CD sold out over the holidays as "Shoop Shoop" parties began springing up from coast to coast.

"Most movies are about men," said one woman. "I'm usually sitting next to my husband, who's saying, 'Yeah!' This is *my* turn."

"I tried to drag my boyfriend to see it," a college student said, "but he wouldn't come. He called it a 'chick' movie. He's a jerk."

The $14-million "chick" movie, released by Twentieth Century–Fox, opened in first place on December 22, 1995, and has ridden a wave of enthusiasm among women everywhere. Some industry executives worried that men wouldn't see it, and sassy females shouted back, "Who cares?"

Fox's president, Robert Harper, said, "The film goes a long way to proving that this audience can drive box office."

For the first time in the history of motion pictures, the main audience was African-American women, who were tired of viewing violent, downbeat 'hood films. They loved seeing themselves in a glossy soap opera portrayed as savvy, successful middle-class women who can get down and dish the dirt.

"Seeing the movie was like going to a really cool slumber party," one fan said. "It's like you were privy to all the inside stuff, the hot jokes and the latest slang. All the actresses were dead-on. I felt like I'd wandered into their heads and was hearing their thoughts spoken aloud."

Whitaker remembers the day Loretta Devine's character was celebrating her birthday and the other actresses were supposed to sing "Happy Birthday" to her but they wouldn't. None of them wanted to trade high notes with Whitney Houston. "I was like, I'm gonna lip-synch," Angela Bassett said. "I'm not singing in front of Whitney."

"Ditto," said Lela Rochon. "At first, I was just mouthing the words, then Forest caught me and yelled, 'Lela, why won't you sing?' "

"Eventually we worked it back and forth," Bassett says. "We all sang a little and she sang a lot."

Rochon went on to say, "There's never been an accurate re-flection on-screen of me and my friends and peers. Hollywood has always overlooked the ordinary and shown African Americans as crackheads or hookers. God bless 'em, but *I* don't know 'em."

In just three weeks, *Exhale* grossed $45 million. Women were going to theaters in large groups, then hanging around in the lobby afterward to discuss it, like at a big party. As if they were emotionally supporting the four actresses, audiences would yell out, "You go, girl!" or, "Work it, baby!"

Producer Deborah Schindler said, "I've heard from several theater managers that people are coming back because they couldn't hear all the dialogue." She and her partner, Ezra Swerd-low, are considering adapting Terry McMillan's 1989 novel, *Disappearing Acts,* to the screen as well.

McMillan enjoyed working with Whitney and said she was "a better actress than she realizes and has great screen presence. All the women were terrific, but Loretta Devine was the most nat-ural. She stole quite a few scenes."

Even though it was an ensemble cast, Whitney's name was the one most closely connected with *Exhale,* and reviewers inevitably began their columns: "Whitney's new movie, *Waiting to Exhale,* has now grossed over $60 million with no end in sight. . . . She is the biggest-selling female artist in the history of music and now a bona fide movie star to boot!"

"You can't really plan fame or what you'll do with it once you have it," Whitney said. "Or how you'll handle it. Or how you'll feel about your audiences. Or how they'll feel about you. I just want to sing. I wish people would concentrate more on my singing than on my life and on my so-called temper. It's my life, my *person,* my moods, and I don't choose to share each and every bit of it with the entire world. I didn't ask for all of this, all this attention and invasion of privacy. They say it comes with the territory—well, I don't think it does. Nor do I think it should have to."

Cissy, who had chased success and fame all of her life, seemed to have had a change of heart. "The price of fame is a great one," she said. "I don't know anymore if it's worth it. I really and truly don't."

"Everything in the whole fuckin' world revolves around my sister," Michael told me one night when we were relaxing in his hotel room. "She's become this big monster star, this *celebrity* who can't even take a pee without some asshole sticking a camera through the window. It's got everybody in the family nuts, man."

We were passing a joint between us and reflecting on some of the wild times we had had together on the road with Whitney, and Michael said, "Remember that time in New York when the limo was surrounded by a dozen fuckin' cops, all of 'em pointing guns at the car?"

"Naw, man," I said. "I wasn't there that night." But I had read about it in the newspaper. It happened in October 1993 when Whitney, along with Bobby, Bobbi Kris, and her usual entourage, were returning form a European tour. As their limo was pulling out of John F. Kennedy Airport, they were suddenly cut off by five squad cars, each one carrying two police officers. The officers, with guns drawn, surrounded the limo and demanded to see some identification. Whitney rolled down her window and told the cop who she was, adding, "My child is in here. Whatever you want, *please* be careful."

Even though a fellow officer had said, "Hey, that really *is* Whitney Houston!" his partner insisted on Whitney's showing her ID. She stayed perfectly calm as she handed over her ID, but the guns remained trained on the occupants in the car until the policeman had satisfied himself that the ID was real. They apologized and drove away, but Whitney was livid. "How could this happen?" she groaned. "My God, this is 1993—*not* 1963!"

"The cops saw a limousine full of blacks," Michael said, "and just automatically figured they were drug dealers or gangsters."

When the truth came out, that's exactly what the officers had thought. The Port Authority Police had been staking out a limousine that was allegedly waiting for the head of a drug cartel to arrive at JFK. "They became confused when they saw Ms. Houston's limousine driving away from the parking lot," a spokesman for Port Authority said. "And they gave pursuit. It was a regrettable error."

John Houston didn't see it that way. He was outraged and said, "Those cops recognized Whitney. And still they didn't drop their guns. If anyone in that car would have made a sudden movement, they would all have been wiped out."

"My license plates say NIPPY, INC, for chrissakes," Whitney fumed. "How many fucking drug lords are named Nippy? They could have killed my baby!"

She stomped down to the police station and demanded to see the official report of the incident, and when she did, she screamed, "Liars!" and ripped it in half. It stated that only two police cars had been involved—and no guns.

Whitney demanded, and got, a public apology. Charles Knox, the NYPD's superintendent of public safety, admitted that "upon further investigation undertaken at my behest, we have found that the initial police reports were erroneous in indicating that only two police officers and two police cars pulled over Ms. Houston's limousine. In fact, we have found that there were at least five police cars and at least nine officers, several of them with weapons drawn, present when the vehicle was stopped."

Michael told me word was on the street that Whitney and Bobby had been set up, that the cops had been told there would be drugs in the limo. "Bobby's made a few enemies in the past," Michael said, "and there's people looking for him."

As much as Whitney claimed to love Bobby, his violent lifestyle and dangerous choice of friends worried her. When her Bentley, a gift from Warner Bros. for the huge success of *The Bodyguard*, was riddled with bullets and her husband's bodyguard was killed, all she could think was, "My baby could have been in that car."

Bobby admitted the shooting had sobered him up "real quick," and an onlooker said, "It was like a shoot-out in a movie, man. The brothers were just leaving the Biarritz [a tough bar in the Orchard Park section of Boston] when bullets started flying. The shooter got Bobby's boy while he was sitting in the car, man, then reached in through the window and stole the gold chain right off his neck! A couple of Bobby's other boys opened fire, but the dude got away."

When the police arrived, Bobby refused to cooperate with them, claiming he didn't even know Sealy. He went back inside the bar but came out a few minutes later and began punching the wall, yelling, "They got my boy!" He followed the ambulance that took Sealy to Boston City Hospital and got into a screaming match with reporters who were trying to cover the story.

"He was running up and down the halls screaming like a madman," one of the nurses said. "When he was told his friend had died, I thought he would tear the place up."

Bobby went into hiding, and when he emerged two weeks later, he checked himself into the Betty Ford Clinic. He told reporters, "I realize I've screwed up, but now I'm trying to get my act together again. I love Whitney, and if there's any way to make up what I put her through, I'm going to try and do it. I realize now I haven't been in control the past three years. It's been drugs and alcohol telling me what to do. I look back now and can't believe it was me doing all that shit."

While Bobby was undergoing treatment, Whitney was trying to keep the Royal Family together and out of the glare of bad publicity. She flatly ordered Cissy, John, Robyn, and Michael not to say a word to anyone about her or Bobby or "any other fucking thing. God, I just wish people would keep their fucking mouths shut and let me live my life!

"Just take all that stress and bullshit and multiply it by a thousand," Michael said. "That's what it's like being around her today. She just goes ballistic sometimes. I think she's going to have a nervous breakdown or some fucking thing unless she gets a grip."

But it was hard to do so when tabloid headlines in the supermarket screamed shocking revelations. The two-page "insider" scoop about Bobby's confession in the Betty Ford Clinic, apparently told to a group of at least thirty other patients, was the most hurtful of all to Whitney. She also learned Bobby had been paid "big bucks" for the personal interview and that he was telling friends he was broke and needed the money. He said Whitney had cut up his credit cards and refused to support him until he got sober.

"That really pissed him off," a member of the Royal Family said, "because he knows she supports everybody else in the family." It's been reported John Houston earns $500,000 per year as her manager, Cissy receives $300,000 as her "adviser," and Robyn rakes in the same amount as her "personal assistant."

The success of *Exhale* demanded more of Whitney's time than she had to give, and she often showed up late for interviews and TV shows. Most often, she and Angela Bassett were scheduled for the same interview, and it wasn't long before reporters began comparing the two. Bassett was always on time, in full makeup, prepared, and ready, but along with photographers, makeup people, and reporters, Bassett was kept waiting for the diva of pop, sometimes up to two hours. Bassett was always unfailingly polite and a pleasure to work with, while Whitney was often rude and arrogant.

On one shoot in Manhattan, Whitney dashed into the studio and disappeared behind the curtain for makeup and wardrobe without even acknowledging the others who had been waiting for her. When she emerged, the public face was in place, frozen, beautiful, closed. After the shoot and a brief interview, Angela Bassett graciously thanked everyone in the studio, but Whitney simply spun on her heel and left—with her entourage hastening to keep up. On the sidewalk, fans rushed her for autographs, but her bodyguards hustled her into her new black Rolls-Royce limousine and sped away.

"They pull her everywhere," Cissy told Jess Cagle. "And she's going through her own personal things right now." She's busier than she's ever been, if that's possible, with a new movie starting in January, new videos, the sound track for *The Preacher's Wife*, traveling, TV and magazine interviews, and trying to spend time with Bobbi Kris. With such a full plate she doesn't need to see her marriage played out in the media.

"It's very difficult," Cissy said. "We all feel what she feels. I know how mean people can be. They want to see you go up, but they like to see you fall, too. Why, I don't know—I just don't know why that is.

Cagle was supposed to do a one-on-one interview with Whitney when she returned to New York, but her publicist called and said Ms. Houston had been ill and was still recuperating at a friend's house in Atlanta. A telephone interview would have to suffice.

"Are you going to write me up right?" Whitney said the moment Cagle called her. "Because I'm telling you something, they've been fucking me up lately." She wanted to talk about her career and said she had no intention of giving up singing for acting because singing has always been her first love, but she admitted she enjoyed working on *Exhale* and was looking forward to her next role.

"Angela should get an Oscar nomination for this," she said. "That girl is amazing. I don't sing a song the same way every night 'cause different emotions come into play. Watching Angela do that in acting with words helped me a lot."

When asked about her troubled marriage, her voice grew stronger and she snapped, "We all have our problems and troubles. All I want to do is be able to work them out in private. They say he cheats on me. I haven't caught him yet. If I had, I'd break his fucking neck. I've got projects coming up for kids that are incredible, for child abuse and things of that nature, but all these people [the media] want to write about is who we're fucking and who we're not fucking and all this other bullshit and I'm tired of it! I know who he comes home to. They write all this shit about me being a lesbian, and one day I'm gonna have to talk to my daughter about it. Please, I'm so pissed off right now. Excuse me."

She left Cagle holding the phone for a few minutes, then came back and said, "I do not share my bed with anybody but my husband. I really, really pray they would stop doing that to me."

Cagle asked what *could* he write about her marriage, and she said, "Nothing. I don't want anybody to know anything because if they do, they start writing more on that. We just want them to think we're still apart. Fuck 'em.'"

She calmed down a little when responding to questions about *Exhale* but demanded to know why there had never been a hit movie about black women or no huge black female stars who could get a multimillion-dollar project produced simply by signing their name. The only actresses who have that kind of clout are white: Demi Moore, Julia Roberts, and Sandra Bullock—with reported salaries of $10–12 million per film. Whitney will join these ranks with *The Preacher's Wife,* where her price for signing is $10 million. It's the first time in the history of motion pictures a black actress has received such a staggering paycheck.

"Remember Dorothy Dandridge?" she asked. "She was a talented, beautiful actress, so much more talented than Marilyn Monroe, but she ended up in obscurity. How come more people don't know about her."

They will if Whitney goes through with her plan of adapting the singer-actress's life story to film. Dandridge was best known for her role in *Porgy and Bess,* but also starred in *Carmen Jones* and *Island in the Sun* with Harry Belafonte. She was beautiful and extraordinarily talented, but fought a losing battle with alcoholism and committed suicide in 1965.

When asked about her quote to *Time* magazine that "white America is fucking with me," she bitterly denied it, saying *Time* had misquoted her, although "I don't know any black people that own *Star* magazine, or any *Enquirer*s or *Vanity Fair*s. Upscale all-black publications like *Ebony, Jet,* and *Essence* all have positive things to say about what Bobby and I do in our personal and professional lives—*not* what we do in our bedroom."

According to a photographer who shot the stills on the Scottsdale, Arizona, location, "The more she refuses to talk to the press, the more they're going to want to know about her. The public has this insatiable interest in everything she does, it's just amazing. While I was there [on location], the first thing anybody asked me was, 'What's Whitney like—is she really a double-barreled bitch, a conceited prima donna, an arrogant diva?' Well, she's none of those things. She was very down-to-earth, very sweet and friendly."

"I think it's the people she surrounds herself with," said another source. "They are not as cultured as she is. They're kind of gruff, crude. But I think that's really her own interior as well. There's something cold and hard about her. She's tough."

"She doesn't want anybody getting too close," said *Exhale* costar Donald Faison. "She was fine in Arizona. She was never mobbed. People would see her and whisper. 'That's Whitney Houston,' and that was it. In New York it would have been a mob scene with fans chanting her name and wanting a piece of her."

Faison went on to say, "She had her daughter with her, and when I'd go, 'Hi, Bobbi,' she'd frown and say, 'I don't know you.' But when Whitney was holding her, she'd always smile at me."

15

A Dream Team

WHEN *WAITING TO EXHALE* CAME TO CHICAGO, I TOOK MY MOTHER and my kid sister to see it. They loved it. "It was like hanging out with my best friends," my sister said. My mother said, "I know all those women. I grew up with women just like that, but it's the first time I've seen them portrayed in a Hollywood movie so perfectly." I enjoyed the movie, too, and could now understand what all the flap was about. The four women had a real bond, and their bawdy humor and joyful air of just-between-us-girls conspiracy made it work. The dreamy, soulful R&B ballads written by Babyface were the best I'd heard in a long time.

Several of my women friends who had read the book said the movie was a faithful adaptation. Terry McMillan had worked on the script herself, sharing writing credit with Ronald Bass (*Rain Man* and *The Joy Luck Club*), and they proved to be an unbeatable team.

Whitney and Bobby spent Christmas 1995 together in her New Jersey mansion, Bobby's first sober holiday in a long while. He told Jamie Foster Brown, publisher of *Sister 2 Sister*, "I feel there's nobody else I'd rather spend the rest of my life with. Through good and bad, sugar. I didn't want to spend another century trying to get to know someone else, once I found the person I like being with and can make me smile just as I can make her smile. She goes after what she wants—she's real. She's real with herself. That's what counts."

Much to everyone's surprise, Whitney embraced the three children Bobby had fathered out of wedlock—Landon, seven, LaPrincia, six, and Robert, three—and encouraged him to see them often. "I love my kids," Bobby told Jamie. "I love them with everything I have in me. They're my strength. They hold me together. They all get along. They're protective of each other."

But when Jamie asked him about the paternity suit pending against him involving a baby girl born in Boston just a few months after his marriage to Whitney, he exploded, "That's bullshit! Women just do that. I'm going to give my blood and show the baby is not mine."

Whitney began shooting *The Preacher's Wife* with Denzel Washington in January while Bobby launched a comeback. A much-anticipated reunion album with his former band, New Edition, was in the works, as well as his first solo LP in three years. Friends rallied around him giving him a strong support system in his battle against the bottle. "We try to keep him busy, keep his mind occupied," one longtime pal said.

TV star Martin Lawrence gave Bobby an important role in his upcoming movie *A Thin Line Between Love and Hate,* and insiders say Bobby's performance was so strong the producers wished his role had been bigger. Critics claimed Bobby was jealous of his wife's soaring career and he had only taken the part in Lawrence's movie to prove that he, too, could act in a film, that it wasn't that damn hard.

"How could I be jealous of my own wife?" he asked Jamie Foster Brown. "That's—how Mike Tyson would say—ludicrous. God has given me too much for me to be jealous of anybody else. It's not me. Not at all. I like it when she does her little thing—her little acting thing. She had fun doing the movie. That's important."

He may not have been envious of his wife's career, but a lot of people told me he was *very* jealous of her new leading man. Forty-one-year-old Denzel Washington has it all, good looks, personality, charm, success, sex appeal, talent, and brains, which only makes trouble-plagued, twenty-six-year-old Bad Boy Bobby look like a punk in comparison.

While filming in New Jersey the two actors became close, and it was obvious to bystanders that Denzel was giving Whitney a lot of emotional support. John Rasario, a bystander who watched them film the scene where they danced in the street, said:

"Whitney only seemed to have eyes for Denzel. She was very shy, even unfriendly with everyone else, but when she was with Denzel, she gazed at him a lot, always with a big, radiant smile. My sister asked if she could have a picture with her, and Whitney turned her down flat—pretty rude, too—but then Denzel came over and took her hand and she was all smiles again."

Waitress Ginny Zhang, who works at the Chan An restaurant, said the film crew used the restaurant as a sort of resting place between takes. "Whitney and Denzel would sit together in a booth and talk for hours sometimes, waiting for the next shot to be set up. They were very low-key, tranquil. Then [director] Penny Marshall would dash into the restaurant and join them for a few minutes. She's a very hyper lady. She'd be chain-smoking and talking a mile a minute, but she seemed happy with how the movie was going."

Another observer, fan Lory Perez, admitted to eavesdropping on the two superstars, hoping to hear some intimate cooing, but she was disappointed. "All they talked about were their families," she said. "I got the feeling that Denzel is very happily married and a great dad, too."

Whitney took a short break from filming to arrange a party for Bobby's birthday, his twenty seventh, at the Mirage nightclub in New York, and *everyone* in the club stopped what they were doing to watch them enter. Whitney was surrounded by her usual entourage and was walking side by side with Robyn Crawford as they were shown to their table. Bobby and his boys hung out in the bar and only came over to Whitney's table once during the evening. As soon as he left, Whitney turned her attention to an unidentified man in her party, and onlookers saw them kiss more than once. Meanwhile, women were swarming around Bobby and his boys, and Whitney didn't even glance in their direction.

As soon as the cake was wheeled out, Bobby sliced it, alone, and a few minutes later he escorted Whitney, Robyn, and their group into a waiting limousine. He returned to the club alone and continued to party with his friends.

In an interview for *Sister 2 Sister* magazine, he said, "I am not being supported by my wife. I am a writer-producer who has a string of hits and receives checks weekly." He also denied that he still resents and dislikes Robyn: "Untrue. Me and Robyn are tight. We have problems because of the fact that she handles my wife's business. There are some things I see that could be handled differently, and I'll speak on it. As far as anything else, no."

He did reluctantly admit to "personality conflicts" in the past, magnified by his drinking, and said he is working on them. "I would go wild and drink and try to wash away what was being said about me, about my wife, my family. But I recognized you can't drink those problems away."

In the meantime, Whitney gave her own, very dignified interview to *Kastle* and refused to discuss anything personal. Asked why she had waited so long between films, she said, "After *The Bodyguard* I had to take a break. It was like I had a new career. I didn't know it was going to be like that. You do a movie, but you don't expect it to be the tenth bestselling movie in the history of all movies or the sound track to be the bestselling of all time. I didn't. I just gave it my best shot and with what I knew and what I learned and what I was absorbing from those around me. But after 'I Will Always Love You' was released and sold a million copies, I knew I was on another ride."

She was asked, "Is there a lot of pressure to maintain the level of success you've achieved?"

"I suppose there could be if I try to outrun it or outdo it, but I don't think that way. I think about doing quality work so therefore I won't run into bad films or consistent bad films."

"It seems you've done so much, is there anything else you want to do?"

"Right now I'm an executive producer. I was executive producer of the last two sound-track albums that I've done. I've written on this one, I've collaborated with one of the greatest producers in the music business to put together one of the greatest sound tracks I think I've heard. I have a production company. I have a record company, and now Disney has developed a deal for me."

The interviewer queried, "Do you ever feel like you have to pick one career over the other?"

"No, not ever. Because I don't do movies back-to-back. I don't want to do movies like that. It's not about doing movies for the sake of doing movies or because it's Hollywood and it's beautiful and glamorous. I want to do great work with great people and that takes time. I pick and choose carefully what I do. Of course, I'm a lot more creative in my own element, which is music, because it's always been my first love."

For the past couple of years, CBS-TV president Peter Tortorici had been planning a remake of the Rodgers and Hammerstein production *Cinderella*, and he wanted Whitney to star. The project was being developed by Storyline Productions, which had had a smash hit with *Gypsy*, starring Bette Midler, in 1993, and they felt *Cinderella* would be equally well received. Especially with the wildly popular diva in the lead. The children's classic had been adapted to the small screen twice in the past, in 1957 with Julie Andrews and in 1965 with Lesley Ann Warren. This would be the first time, ever, that the fairy-tale princess would be played by a black woman.

As one TV executive said, "If you want the most beautiful and famous black princess in the world, there's only one choice: Whitney Houston."

However, as with every project offered to Whitney, it would have to wait until her schedule was free before meetings could begin. And her schedule, as usual, was full. She took a brief time out from filming her movie to attend the Soul Train Music Awards, where she picked up a statue for Best Female Single for "Exhale (Shoop Shoop)," and she was seen again at the thirty-eighth annual Grammy Awards.

Wearing a skintight, floor-length gown of royal burgundy, with just a glimmer of leg seen through the almost transparent fabric, her hair in ringlets, she headlined a salute to gospel music and told the crowd she was "very proud to be here to honor the music that gave me my roots." After introducing Cece Winans, she stood in the wings for a few minutes before rejoining her in a rousing gospel number that brought the audience to its feet. Huge diamonds sparkled on both hands, her teeth flashed like pearls, and her voice soared as she tore into the foot-stomping rendition with Cece. A full choir, decked out in long flowing robes, clapped and swayed behind the two divas as the crowd wend wild, whistling, cheering, and yelling for more.

In a much quieter moment, Bobby took the stage dressed in a white tux and introduced R&B vocalist Shirley Caesar. It was crystal clear who the star was that night—and it didn't set well with Bobby.

"They seemed to be getting along okay," said a bystander who witnessed Whitney and Bobby together backstage. "Whitney was talking with her mother and happened to glance over and see Bobby in a huddle with rap star Tupac Shakur, and she went ballistic, man. She marched over and grabbed Bobby by the collar and literally dragged him away. They were both screaming at each other, and she was accusing him of being up to his old ways and he was yelling that she had embarrassed him in front of his boys."

Tupac Shakur is a convicted sex offender and well-known drug user, so Whitney "thought Bobby was trying to score some dope," a member of her party told stunned onlookers. Tupac and Bobby used to hang out together, but on that night Bobby insisted he had just wanted to talk to him about writing a song for

Tupac's new film. The loud arguing continued until the doors of their limo closed and they sped back to their hotel. They left L.A. the next day.

When Whitney returned to work on *The Preacher's Wife,* Bobby was with her. "He sort of just hung around," one of the crew members said. "He seemed at loose ends and just wandered aimlessly around the set, hardly bothering to watch the shooting. Except when his wife had a romantic scene with Denzel, then he moved closer and paid strict attention."

Cast and crew had flown to Deering Oaks, Maine, a quaint, picturesque little town, for the scene where the two stars skate together on a romantic village pond and Whitney's character realizes she's attracted to Denzel's character. An unexpected warm spell had partially melted the ice, however, so many of the scenes had to be reshot several times. The actors were trying to look graceful while two inches of water crept up their ankles.

Denzel was by far the most confident on skates and had to scoop Whitney up more than once when she took a spill. They did their own skating for the close-ups, but doubles stepped in for the fancy footwork. When asked how he was getting along with his costar, Denzel said, "Whitney is very talented and great to work with. It's great working on this set. Everyone gets along so well."

Penny Marshall endeared herself to local merchants when she spent over $50,000 on antiques, then hit the outlet stores looking for more bargains. Bobby kept a low profile and was solicitous toward his wife.

The following week, when the tabloids hit the stands, an article hinted of a hot romance brewing between the two stars, and a friend told me Robyn had planted the item. "She's still trying to break them up," he said. "She thinks if she can get Bobby jealous enough, he'll take a walk. He's a feisty little dude with a *big* ego, and he wouldn't stand for his wife cheating on him."

I was also told Robyn was not at all happy with her boss's marriage, even though she had consistently told the press she was, and when she wasn't depressed, she was sullen and brooding. Michael told me Robyn never thought Whitney would take her relationship with Bobby this far and she was determined to get her back. "Those two have been going at each other's throat since they were kids," Michael said. "It's always a contest, a one-upmanship to see who will back down first. They're both tough as hell, as you well know, and we're just waiting to see who kills who first!"

This wasn't the first time I had heard that friends and family were worried that the close relationship would end up violently. Cissy had always predicted that somebody would kill Robyn, while other family members were afraid Robyn would kill Whitney *and* herself. From my firsthand experience with them, I had to agree. Trouble was brewing, and in time it would boil over and scald everybody in the Royal Family. And I was glad I wasn't there any longer so I wouldn't get caught in the mayhem.

16

The Day Nelson Mandela Was Kept Waiting

PRAISE CONTINUED TO BE HEAPED UPON WHITNEY AND HER PERformance in *Waiting to Exhale*. One critic claimed the main reason for anyone to see this movie was because of the many beautiful close-ups of the queen of pop.

Entertainment Weekly magazine devoted an entire page just to her hairstyles over the past few years. "She's gone light, dark, curly, softer curls, ringlets," said her hairstylist, Ellin La Var. "She's done anything and everything you could imagine to her hair." In *Exhale* the new, updated shag is sleeker and more natural. Said her makeup artist, Kevyn Aucoin, "I used an apricot color on her cheeks and golden warm brown tones on her eyes and brows. I went for a sort of burgundy for the lips. The contrast brings forward the perfection of her teeth."

Said another makeup artist, "With that fabulous face, she could go completely bald and still be a knockout!"

181

Even though Bobby was on the set during his wife's scenes with Denzel, rumors persisted that "sparks are flying hot and heavy between the two most beautiful black actors in Hollywood. . . . They will have trouble convincing their mates they're just acting."

In an interview with Lynn Norment for *Ebony*, Denzel admitted the attention was flattering. He described a recent evening when he was presenting an award and walked into the huge, celebrity-packed ballroom with his wife, Pauletta Pearson. "When we came in, it was like the whole room tilted and everybody fell over toward us. People got up and were knocking tables and chairs down. They had to get bodyguards and all kinds of stuff. It was wild!"

He was amazed that people could get so excited by his presence, especially such as upper-echelon group. "I mean, it's flattering, it's great. Trust me, I'm not complaining, but I feel for my wife in situations like that. She gets jostled around because people are enthusiastic. It's not that they are trying to knock her down or hurt me or anything. It just becomes crowd madness."

He can relate to Whitney's prickly attitude toward the press. "You don't have your privacy as much," he said. "You don't feel free to just walk around. People want to use you or get something from you. You can't trust as much as you once did."

At six feet tall with perfect, classic features, he is considered the most handsome black man in movies today. He is also one of Hollywood's top-grossing leading men, whose bankable cinematic presence can carry a film all by itself. When asked about his sex appeal and women's swooning at the sight of his gorgeous face, he shrugs it off with boyish charm. "That's what people might say about me, but that's not who I am. Whatever gifts I have been given—I work from the inside out, not the outside in. I'm not a look. I'm an actor. When I first started out twenty years ago, there was nobody saying I was a sex symbol, good-looking, all that stuff. Maybe I just matured well."

And what about all the rumors of a romance brewing between him and Whitney? "Pure gossip," he says. "I'm a family man. I love my wife and kids." Friends say he is a devoted, hands-on father to his children—an eleven-year-old son, seven-year-old daughter, and five-year-old twins (a boy and girl)—as well as a loving and faithful husband.

Along with the glowing accolades Whitney was receiving, she was also getting some criticism for her acid-tongued remarks to reporters. Jonathan Edwards of Rochester, New York, wrote in response to Jess Cagle's Internet interview, "Number of times Whitney Houston said the F-word in your interview: six. Number of times she says the S-word: three. I am not waiting for further exhalations."

"Reading your article on these two stellar women, I found myself wanting to learn more about Angela Bassett and less about Whitney Houston," wrote Scott Barrow of Westwood, New Jersey. "Bassett seems a true professional, warm, intelligent, and poised. Houston sounded like she was rehearsing for an appearance on Letterman."

Sally Harmon of Los Angeles, California, wrote, "Whitney Houston needs an attitude adjustment. She wants us to believe she's this holier-than-thou, churchgoing 'good' girl, then cusses like a guttersnipe. In every interview I've read, she uses the F-word constantly."

Perhaps embarrassed about the way her salty language was getting too much press, Whitney made a statement that *Time* magazine had misquoted her as saying, "White America tried to fuck with me." However, *Time* writer Christopher John Farley had recorded his interview with her: she was correctly quoted.

Whitney's publicist, Lois Smith, was kept busy denying reports about her boss's bad behavior in public and trying to play down that Whitney was rude and arrogant to the very people who made her so famous. She often referred to her middle-class black fans as "ghetto bitches" and "nigs"—I have personally heard her use these slurs dozens of times—and would wither them with "the look" if they got too close. But even Smith couldn't quiet the outcry against Whitney when she kept Nelson

Mandela waiting for almost two hours for a meeting with him at the White House.

While the Royal Family was "categorically denying" every piece of bad press against Whitney, they brought up the story about "a would-be hit man claiming he was hired by Whitney's father, John, to break the legs of Robyn Crawford, Houston's executive assistant and longtime friend." I laughed like hell when I read that, since I was the "would-be hit man" and John had indeed tried to hire me to rough up Robyn. When he saw that I couldn't be bought, he quickly turned it into "a joke—Kevin knew I was just kidding around, letting off steam," then he told Robyn to give me as many tickets as I wanted to a concert Whitney was giving in Rosemont, Illinois.

Even though Whitney continued to tell reporters she "didn't take as much shit as she used to," she also saw the wisdom in toning down her anger and had this to say in a *McCall's* magazine interview: "Really, it [my life] has nothing to do with business whatsoever. It's my family. To raise children. To raise decent human beings. To keep my husband happy. To keep him strong. Things of that nature. They are very simple things."

She told insiders she was going to make this marriage work no matter what because she wanted another baby, maybe two, and "Bobby makes the prettiest babies."

In March 1996, she agreed to do the Rodgers and Hammerstein musical *Cinderella,* telling the studio it would be "a gift for my daughter, Bobbi Kris." Writer Robert Freedman has already finished the modernized version, and CBS producer Neil Meron says, "Cinderella will not be a victim as she was in the old tale. She won't be admired by the prince just because she's good-looking. In the new version, she's evolved."

When I read about Whitney's signing to play Cinderella, I was blown away. Not just because it was Whitney, but because it was a black woman in the role of a blond-haired, blue-eyed, lily-white princess. I thought, *Old Walt Disney must be spinning in his grave.* I couldn't think of any fairy tales with a black person as the central character except "Little Black Sambo" and "Uncle

Remus," so I was thrilled for Whitney. I wished I could pick up the phone and call her and ask how she felt about it. I wished I could relax with her as I used to do and swap childhood stories, but I knew that was impossible. She had more security around her than President Clinton. In the two short years since I had been with her, she had become so incredibly famous, it was almost as if I had never known her.

Knowing how she felt about fame and the constant invasion of her privacy, I felt sorry for her and wished I could comfort her in some way. "I never wanted fame," she told me on several occasions. "My mother wanted fame, but I just wanted to sing." I remembered when I had first met her. She was so warm and friendly, so open about her life. We would talk for hours about how similar our childhoods were and how far we had both come from such humble beginnings.

Whitney's early childhood was poor and lonely and she told me she always wished her mother had been around more. She didn't understand Cissy's hunger for fame—and now that she's so famous herself, she understands it even less. How a mother could leave her small children alone night after night while she chased after a dream seemed unconscionable. Perhaps that's why Whitney is such a good mother herself and rarely lets Bobbi Kris out of her sight.

I know all the hype in the press about what a strong, supportive, Christian family life Whitney had and how she adores her parents and gives them full credit for her success, but when I was with her, I saw it much differently. She was resentful and hostile toward her parents, especially Cissy, and she made it clear who was the boss in the Royal Family. She would tell everyone, "I'm the goose who lays the golden egg, and don't *nobody* ever forget it!"

Michael once told me, "My sister expects everyone to kiss her ass, and they do, too, because she'd fire them in a second if they didn't—even Mom and Dad." More than one member of the staff at Nippy, Inc. has said, "Without Whitney, Cissy and John would be on welfare. He's old and sick and going blind, but she still pays him half a million dollars a year. And Cissy is living like a queen in a New Jersey town house with a spectacular view of the Manhattan skyline. The decor is all white with a white baby grand piano and mirrored walls that reflect the panoramic view of the city sprawled below. Cissy has transformed herself into this soft-spoken, genteel lady of the manor, and it's really a hoot to those of us who know her."

I tried to compare that picture with my memories of Cissy when I knew her. She was hotheaded and opinionated, still believing *she* was the greatest singer of all time. She had always claimed her voice was better than that of any other female singer on earth, including her daughter, which made me wonder why she had never attained stardom or even a lasting success in the music business. Then she was capable of bullying everyone around her, just as John was, but now time had robbed them of that power. Their daughter had become a successful and popular entertainer not because of anything they had ever done for her, but because the world had embraced her.

I would have given a piece of my soul for even a small part of that kind of success. Thinking about Whitney, I both loved and hated her. I was hurt and angry that she'd lied to me about her willingness to help me with my music career. I hadn't gone to her asking for a chance; she'd come to me and offered me one. That night at the Black Achievement Awards when Patti LaBelle had expressed interest in handling me, Whitney had told her in so many words to back off, *she* was my manager. She didn't need to do that. She led me to believe that she was serious when all along it was a control thing with her. If I knew then what I know now, I would have followed Patti and signed with her.

In retrospect, what hurts even more than being lied to by Whitney was that I had bared my soul to her on many occasions and she knew how deeply I felt about becoming a success so I could give my family a better life. She knew how tough my early years had been, and she had sympathized with me and shown a great compassion and understanding. I can still see the warmth and empathy in her eyes when I would talk about the hard times all of us kids, my bothers and sisters, had growing up in the projects with an alcoholic father.

Not only did I hear gunshots daily in the street outside my front door, but I remember one time when my father put a round of shots into that same door. He was drunk and arguing with my mother and just suddenly started shooting into the door. Wood splinters flew in all directions, a few of them embedding themselves in my mother's legs, then he calmly went outside and sat down on the porch. He used to spend a lot of time on the porch, drinking and shouting obscenities at everyone who passed by. Which was a damn foolish thing to do, given the kind of tough street we lived on. I used to worry that someday someone was going to come up on our porch and knock the hell out of my dad for the filthy things he yelled at them.

When we moved into our apartment on Sixty-third Street in Chicago, three murders were committed in the first three weeks we were there; two cabdrivers were killed and another man was shot in the head as he drove by the corner of Fifty-eighth and Green, just blocks from our home. I heard the shots and saw the car crashing into the icehouse fence.

While attending Tilden High School, I joined the music class with the hope of learning to play the saxophone so I could be as famous as my cousin Gene "Jug" Ammons. It was impossible to concentrate as race riots were going on every day. White people, children and adults alike, would stand across the street from my school at Forty-eighth and Union and throw bricks at the black students as they entered the building. The kids would be bleeding and crying, screaming, running like hell to get inside the building, and once we were all inside, the teachers would lock the doors and tend to our wounds. It was a difficult way to get an education.

After school, it was just as bad. There would always be a gang of white boys waiting for us, and they would chase us down the street on their bikes or skates, siccing their dogs and throwing things at us. Those three blocks from school to home seemed more like three miles to me.

187

I told Whitney how I had joined St. Martin's Church of Christ and started singing with the choir because I felt safe there, and she said she understood because she'd always felt safe and less lonely when she went to church as a child. We had both been given solos when we were just youngsters and had been applauded by the entire congregation for the power and beauty of our voices.

When Whitney and I shared these stories, I felt such a warm kinship with her and I truly believed she was my guardian angel. I just *knew* that through her I would realize my dream. That's why I put up with so much for so long from the Royal Family. That's why I didn't knock John on his ass for even suggesting that I would be capable of breaking another human being's arms and legs and take money for it.

My father died when I was fifteen, and things went from very bad to much, much worse. We had always been poor, living on the pittance my father earned when he was able to work, but now we were broke. All the utilities were shut off and it was winter, so we almost froze to death. The water pipes burst and we had to borrow drinking water from the lady next door. My older brother joined the Marines so he wouldn't have the responsibility of being the breadwinner for our large family, and that made me "man of the house." I wanted to quit school and get a full-time job, but my mother wouldn't let me. She insisted that an education was more important than anything else.

Somehow we made it through the winter, and with the warm days of summer, life seemed to look better to us. One day I saw a guy about my age singing on the street corner and I befriended him. We formed a group with a couple of other musicians called Windy City and started hitting all the local talent shows. We won every contest we entered, and people were telling us how great we were and that it was just a matter of time before we were discovered.

We got a gig at the 1125 Club on Fifty-ninth and May Streets and soon had a loyal following—mostly women who screamed and went crazy every time we walked onstage. Our show lasted about two hours, and for this we were paid barely enough to eat, but we didn't complain because we all knew that success was right around the corner. We all thought a talent scout or agent or record producer would come into the club some night and be so impressed, he would sign us on the spot.

One night I was looking out into the audience, and for the first time I realized what a dive the club was. It was a dingy, rat-infested hole-in-the-wall where the customers got drunk and got into brawls and the cops were called but never showed up. No agent or record producer was going to risk going into such a dangerous bar—no matter how good the singing group was.

I consoled myself thinking that I'd gotten a lot of experience and had been able to make a few extra dollars from time to time. Summer was almost over and my mother was determined we would be out of our run-down apartment before winter set in. I don't know where she got the money, but we moved to Forty-eighth and Indiana, which was known in the neighborhood as "the whore strip," and we became virtual prisoners in our own home. My mother wouldn't let any of us kids go outside and play because of the danger. We would look through our window and see hookers being beat up by their pimps. They were kicked and punched and left lying in their own blood until they finally re-gained consciousness and dragged themselves home.

When I turned seventeen, we moved again, this time to Sixty-first and Wolcott, into a house that was given to us by my brother's baseball coach. The coach said we could live in the house rent free in exchange for my brother's services as a pitcher for his semipro baseball team. Even though the house was small and had no electricity, we felt blessed that we had a roof over our heads. We had the gas hooked up illegally and there was water, but sitting in the dark night after night drove me crazy. I would go out to different supermarkets in the neighborhood and steal food to feed my family, and I didn't think it was wrong, it was just necessary.

I was under so much pressure and stress that I started hanging out with the gangs and getting into fights. I felt better after I had kicked somebody's ass, and I liked the respect I got from the other guys. I developed a reputation as the "bone crusher," and people would cross the street when they saw me coming. I was big and husky and could take a guy out with one punch. Everyone knew if they rubbed me the wrong way, I would break their jaw.

I was like the mayor of my neighborhood, highly respected, feared, and also well liked. Girls always made a fuss over me, and the guys wanted to hang with me and be my friend. People would give me stuff, gifts and things, just to let me know they were on my side. I knew it was wrong to hurt people. My mother hadn't raised me that way. But I had so much rage inside me, and I sure as hell wasn't going to run away anymore. If I ran away from some guy one day, I would just have to face him again the next day. I found it was better to get it over with, then try to get along with the guy.

This tactic always worked because nobody wanted to get their nose busted twice by the same guy.

One day when I was hanging out on the street as usual, I saw my brother and a cousin of ours standing out on the porch talking to an attractive girl. They motioned me to come over, then introduced me to their friend Marsha Collins. It was love at first sight. We've now been married for ten years, but we've been together for eighteen years, ever since the first time we saw each other.

Marsha is completely responsible for turning my life around. If I had stayed in the gangs, I'd either be dead or in prison, but her love and strength gave me hope again. She believed in me and believed in my talent as a singer, and so I started writing songs again. Instead of gang-banging with my boys at night, I would stay home with Marsha and rehearse. When I wasn't singing or writing, we would talk, sometimes all night long. I told her all about my youth in the crime-ridden Robert Taylor

Projects and how I had felt responsible for my six sisters and four brothers after my father's death, and she understood. She told me to take that rage and put it into my music, and when I did, everyone sat up and took notice.

All of a sudden people from all over town wanted me to sing at weddings, graduations, church affairs—everywhere! Women went wild, screaming, throwing their panties onstage, tossing roses at me, trying to tear my clothes off. I got countless telephone numbers every time I sang someplace, but I didn't need them. I had the woman I wanted.

My mother had always told me preparation is the key to success—being ready to run through the door whenever it opened, even the slightest crack. And so I began preparing myself for that moment.

In 1980 I had the opportunity to go to Memphis, Tennessee, to perform for the legendary soul-gospel singer the Reverend Al Green in his beautiful church. It was a fantastic experience and the reverend said he was impressed with my singing. He told me I had a great voice and asked me if I would remain in Memphis and sing in his church. I was tempted, but my roots were in Chicago and I really needed to make it there. My mother had always been a big fan of Al Green's so I asked if he would give her a call and just say hello as it would mean the world to her. He readily agreed and was so sweet and charming to my mother I will always be in his debt.

After such a wonderful compliment from Mr. Green, my confidence soared and I was more determined than ever to break into the music world. I rehearsed constantly and wrote songs, and my group and I would perform anywhere at the drop of a hat. We entered every single contest we heard about and won every one. Our reputation as up-and-coming musicians was growing, and we got the usual buzz from shady characters who wanted us to pay for "management." They promised us fame and fortune, for a price. At first, we all fell for it. We knew we were good, but we were just kids and didn't understand that unscrupulous types were out there just looking to take our money and shatter our dreams.

Then we met Lou Rawls's brother, Julius, and thought we had made it this time. He loved our singing style and promised us he would introduce us to Lou the next time the star was in town. All he wanted in return was for us to appear, free of charge, on his shows. We had no problem with that. We loved to perform, and the thought that we would soon meet Lou Rawls was enough incentive to keep us going. When the meeting never took place, I questioned one of Julius's associates and was told that Julius and Lou were not on speaking terms and had not been in touch for a long time. It was a big disappointment, but I tried to turn it into a positive experience; we'd gotten stage exposure and we had learned more about our craft.

One day my brothers and I were walking down the sidewalk, singing just for the pure pleasure of it, when an elderly man stopped and listened, then introduced himself as Paul Bascomb. He said he was a manager and would like to handle us. Of course we were skeptical at this point, but he insisted we go back to his apartment with him so he could get to know a little bit about us.

The apartment was small and shabby, and we were beginning to feel as if this were just another scam and any minute now the old dude would ask us for money. To my amazement, he didn't. He took out a scrapbook–photo album and showed us pictures of him with a variety of stars and articles calling him the "best horn player in the world."

I had written a song for the mayor of Chicago called "Let's Make Chicago Jane Byrne's Town," and Paul loved it and wanted to record it. He found investors to pay for studio time, then started a label with us called H.P. Productions (*H.P.* stood for Herman Powell, the moneyman behind the company). We were also given our own publishing company, Kosy Music, which was set up by attorney Linda Mensche, the same attorney I introduced to Regina years later.

Paul took us to Smokey Joe's, a nice men's shop in Chicago,

and outfitted us with two dress suits per man, with matching ties, pocket handkerchiefs, socks, shoes. We felt, and looked, like stars.

We met at Lake Recording Company in Maywood, Illinois, to cut the record. It was our first time in a twenty-four-track recording studio and we were all impressed. Seventy-two hours later we had our first record with the song for Mayor Jane Byrne on one side and "Ain't Love Heavy?" on the flip side.

We were featured on *The Dave Baum Show* in Chicago and were soon performing at a variety of local functions. We played a number of schools and were paid by the City of Chicago, but soon discovered that our friend and manager, Paul, was pocketing most of the money. So it was back to square one.

Luckily, we had gained a respectful reputation and were in demand as the opening act for top-name groups that appeared at the Burning Spear. I was recognized everywhere I went, and people were always asking me to sing for this function or that party. I wasn't making very much money, but I was doing what I loved: singing. Several times it was suggested to me that I go solo, but I couldn't leave my brothers behind. We had started out together and I wanted us to stay together.

However, a couple of years later, one of my brothers joined the service and it broke the group up, so I finally did go solo. I was in demand as an opening act and also as a backup singer for recording sessions, so I was doing all right, even though I still wasn't making much money.

In 1982, I joined up with Farod Lewis, a young rapper. I wasn't into rap, but I soon became Farod's bodyguard and traveled with him to his various gigs. He started a recording studio called Pushing Wax and we flew to Miami, Florida, to meet with the vice president of Joey Boy Records, Allen Johnson. We knew we would need distribution as well as promotion, and Allen was the man to see. He sent us to New York to meet with Steve Manning, a promoter for the Jackson Five.

I didn't sing on that album as it was all rap, but while I was in New York, I met a guy who was good friends with L. L. Cool J, and he invited me out to Long Island to meet him. L. L. and I hit it off instantly, and that friendship survives today. He wasn't comfortable being called by his stage name and asked me to call him Todd.

I had a great time in New York hanging out with such big stars as L. L. Cool, Kids 'n Play, Russell Simmons, and Heavy D.—I couldn't wait to cut my own album so I could feel like an equal with those guys, and I started working on it as soon as I returned to Chicago. But it was always something! Farod Lewis was arrested and thrown into prison for tax evasion, and there went the recording studio and all my dreams.

17

"Fame Doesn't Make You More Popular"

BY 1990 I WAS NO LONGER A WIDE-EYED KID DREAMIN' THE DREAM about stardom. In the past few years I had seen firsthand how hard it was to break into the music business. It wasn't about being a good singer, it was about politics and inside wheeling and dealing. If a record producer owed another producer a favor, he might bargain for, say, a single by L. L. Cool J, but he would have to give a shot to his new client Kevin Ammons. New people trying to get a break into the business were treated like pawns; they were expendable because a thousand more were always waiting in the wings for that big break.

I was in my thirties now, with a wife and family, and couldn't afford to wait for a break that might never come. I got ahold of some property in Chicago and opened a beauty salon, Billie Jean's, and also a little restaurant next door. I had a steady income and I satisfied my love for music by going to every concert that came to the Chicago area. When I read in the newspaper that Natalie Cole was scheduled to appear at the Drury Lane Theater, I called to find out about getting tickets and that's when I met Regina Brown and my life was turned upside down.

We met in the fall of 1990 and ten months later I was dancing with Whitney Houston in a London nightclub. If anyone would have told me that I'd be holding the most beautiful singing star in the world in my arms, I would have accused them of tripping on LSD.

I was in London as a sort of unofficial bodyguard for Whitney, and she had asked me to escort her to Piccadilly Park where she would speak to a group of children with AIDS. Regina was supposed to write her speech but couldn't do it, and I ended up writing it.

Later that evening we went to a party in Whitney's honor at the Hippodrome, and as we entered the smoky club, it was blasting with loud music. No one made a move toward Whitney or rushed her for autographs or squealed her name as they do in the States. They simply stood and stared. She was holding my arm and her grip tightened as I led her to a table. The club had a smoke machine that caused a dense foglike mist to encircle the dance floor, and when Whitney stepped out in the center to dance with someone, I almost lost sight of her in all the swirling smoke. It made me a little nervous because anything could happen to her out there and nobody would be able to see a thing.

I went to the DJ's booth and asked him to turn the smoke machine down, which he did. As I was returning to our table, Whitney stopped me and asked what was going on. I explained I was worried about her safety in all the thick fog, and she smiled and squeezed my arm, saying, "Thank you, Kevin. What in the fuck do I pay these assholes [her bodyguards] for, anyway? They can't think of anything!" Then she grabbed my hand and tugged me onto the dance floor.

At first I tried to be cool, just dancing politely and rather sedately, but the music was hot and Whitney was hotter, doing all the right moves and smiling right into my eyes. So I started popping my hips, wiggling, moving down close to the floor, really getting into it. I swung around and was shaking my ass with my back to Whitney, and when I spun back around, she was gone! I saw her across the room, dancing with her band director, Ricky Minor. I felt embarrassed and humiliated to be left standing in the middle of the dance floor by myself.

Several seconds passed but it seemed much longer as I stood there sort of moving my feet to the music, then I saw Whitney dancing back toward me and I just turned and walked off the floor. I wanted to show her how it felt to be left alone in the middle of a dance. It was rude and I wasn't going to stand for it, no matter that she was Whitney Houston.

I was standing at the bar having a drink when I heard the sound of high heels clicking across the hardwood floor, heading straight toward me. I didn't turn around. I felt someone touch my hand and it was Whitney. She asked me what was the matter and I told her I didn't like being left standing by myself in the middle of a dance floor.

"Oh, baby," she said. "I'm sorry. Were you jealous because I was dancing with Ricky? Was I being bad?"

"No. Just rude." I walked off the dance floor, leaving her standing there alone looking totally shocked. People were staring at both of us, but I didn't care. The way I saw it, Miss Whitney needed a lesson in good manners.

As much as I admired and even loved Whitney during the time I spent with the Royal Family, one thing about her I just couldn't abide. She openly, and often, showed disrespect to her mother in front of anyone who happened to be around. My own mother raised all ten of us kids to show her respect, no matter what. So when I would see and hear Whitney disrespecting Cissy, it really bothered me. I felt sorry for Cissy, but after a while I realized that it didn't upset her nearly as much as it bothered me. She would just shrug it off, not showing any emotion. I guess she was used to it.

The phenomenal success of *Waiting to Exhale* continued through the winter and spring of 1996. Oprah Winfrey devoted two hour-long shows to its cast members and told her audience the black women of America needed more movies like *Exhale,* movies that showed African Americans in a positive light. She is now developing Toni Morrison's 1987 novel, *Beloved,* into a movie, and dozens of other successful black entertainers are getting projects ready for the big screen.

Even so, they may not reach movie theaters soon enough for an audience that's finally been noticed and is hungry for more attention.

At a recent interview published on the Internet, Whitney was asked how she was handling the huge success of *Exhale* and how she had prepared for her role.

"Angela [Bassett] taught me a lot of things," she said. "Like, if we did a scene four times, Angela would take that one line in the script and change it four different ways. But that's an actress. This girl is a drama student from Yale, she ain't playin'. Me, I'm walkin' in and doing the same scenes and I'm lost. But if I take a song and I do a line, I don't sing it the same way every time. I get satisfaction out of that, the same way Angela gets satisfaction out of twisting her lines different ways."

She was asked, "How do you feel when you see yourself on-screen?"

"With *The Bodyguard,* it took me a long time to be able to look at myself—so I didn't enjoy it until about three years ago. I was on tour and it was on and I watched it for the first time as an observer, and not someone who's in it, and I actually cried at the end."

"Have you been offered a star on the Hollywood Walk of Fame yet?"

Whitney replied, "Let me tell you about that Hollywood Walk of Fame stuff. I have my reservations about that. I heard you got to pay for that mess and someone has to submit you in order to have it. First of all, Hollywood Boulevard is really dirty and I don't want nobody walking on my name! I'm kidding. I'd rather wait until I'm really old—or gone. Give it to my daughter. Let her put it there."

The interviewer inquired whether dealing with fame proved difficult.

"Fame is always the hard part," Whitney replied. "James Taylor said it best: 'Fame and fortune are a curious game—perfect strangers call you by name.' That line does it for me, that's the fame part. The singing and performing is the great part—when people respond the way they do and go out and buy your stuff and want to see you. That means the world to you. That means everything you put into it was worth it."

"What keeps you grounded?"

"I believe in prayer and I believe it changes things and makes a difference in your life. The closer connection you have to God, the closer you are to yourself and able to live with yourself and at least be able to find some happiness."

"It's hard to imagine you ever have problems."

"That's bull! Money doesn't solve problems, it creates them. Fame doesn't make you more popular, it makes people more dangerous. You get people that love you so much they hate you. What kind of shit is that? When all I want to do is sing. It's crazy!"

However, fame and fortune *does* have its perks. In a recent "Insider" column in *People* magazine, reporter Mitchell Fink said, "With mouth agape, I watched Whitney Houston and Barbara Davis, wife of billionaire oilman Marvin Davis, compare outsize diamond rings during the pre-Grammy party thrown by Arista Records president Clive Davis (no relation to Marvin) at the Beverly Hills Hotel. Houston's twelve-carat ring, nice as it was, looked like a frozen pea beside Davis's forty-three-carat boulder."

When I read that, I thought, a twelve-carat diamond—"nice"? My God, the cost of that bauble would feed my family for many, many years!

On April 6, the 27th Annual NAACP Image Awards was held inside the Pasadena Civic Auditorium in California before a crowd of over three thousand guests. After a quarter of a century, the Image Awards, for positive portrayals in the arts of African

Americans, have finally made it to prime time. "This is *our* Oscars," said comic Sinbad.

Denzel Washington and Whitney hosted the event, which celebrated the contributions of African Americans to television, film, music, and literature. Whitney slithered onstage in a silver lamé gown that clung to every sensational curve, giving her the look of a goddess come to life. Denzel held his own next to her in a dark Armani suit, white, collarless dress shirt, silver-gray satin tie, and matching pocket handkerchief.

The show opened with the hip-hop version of "Killing Me Softly With His Song" by the Fugees, then was followed by a warm salute to Quincy Jones by Ray Charles and blues artist Ernestine Anderson, who performed "Let the Good Times Roll." Jones took home an award for Entertainer of the Year.

Denzel Washington snagged Best Actor for his dramatic performance in *Crimson Tide,* and Angela Bassett won Best Actress for *Waiting to Exhale.* "I wanted to be comfortable yet gorgeous," she joked, referring to her clingy, black Badgley Mischka gown. "*Now* I can exhale!"

Denzel thanked his wife and family: "She [Pauletta] gives me a hundred percent—a hundred and ten percent support in everything I do."

The audience included Oprah Winfrey (stunning in a blue Valentino gown), Alfre Woodward, Queen Latifah, Victoria Rowell, Jada Pinkett (in a creamy silk suit), Will Smith, Malik Yoba, Martin Lawrence, Arsenio Hall, Richard Pryor, Brandy, Lynn Whitfield (in white satin and black net), Jaleel White, Coolio, and many more. They screamed their approval as *Waiting to Exhale* breezed easily to seven awards, including Best Actress; Best Picture, Forest Whitaker director; Outstanding Female Artist, Whitney Houston for "Exhale (Shoop Shoop)"; Outstanding Album the Year, producers Babyface and Clive Davis.

"There's a lot of deals being made here tonight," Robert Townsend [*Hollywood Shuffle*] said, gesturing toward Oprah Winfrey, who was in a business huddle with a *Living Single* star, rapper Queen Latifah.

Whitney held her own mini–fashion show by changing gowns at least four times. After her first appearance in the silver lamé, she returned wearing a tight black number with a black mesh, see-through bodice with high neck and long sleeves, then another black gown with a straight skirt and skinny spaghetti straps, and finally yet *another* black gown, this one with a clingy halter top and diamond choker. The back was cut down to the waist with a diamondlike tassel that just brushed her buttocks. When she took center stage to sing "Exhale (Shoop Shoop)," the crowd went wild, giving her a standing ovation.

However, they were respectfully silent when Arsenio Hall presented Richard Pryor (wheelchair bound with multiple sclerosis) with a Hall of Fame special award.

The finale was a rousing, hand-clapping gospel number performed by Kurt Franklin and Family with the Crenshaw Choir, and about midway through, Whitney joined them to more audience approval. Then Gregory Hines danced onstage to join Whitney, and one of the biggest galas of the year was over.

Onlookers backstage said Whitney was beaming from ear to ear and hugged Angela Bassett several times, telling her, "I just *knew* you'd win, girl!" She was also seen embracing Denzel for his win and again congratulating Forest Whitaker on the awards sweep of *Waiting to Exhale*—but no one could recall seeing Bobby Brown anywhere.

"I think he was here," a stagehand said, "but I can't say for sure."

While his wife was racking up awards and accolades, Bobby was making his debut on the big screen, costarring with his old pal Martin Lawrence in *A Thin Line Between Love and Hate*. When asked by *People* magazine reporter Kim Cunningham if the title conveys a concept familiar to Bobby, he said, "Most definitely, when it comes to relationships, there can be a thin line between love and hate. I don't want to talk about my personal life except to say I've been blessed. Whitney and I are on solid ground. We're together. We love our little daughter. We like to watch her get up every morning. She's learning to dance. I'm not really teaching her, though, because dancing is in her genes. She's something else—a small Whitney with a big Bobby flair!"

The comedy also stars the beautiful Lynn Whitfield, Della Reese, and Roger E. Mosley. It did not get good reviews except, surprisingly, for Bobby Brown. Critics have praised his performance as "Tee" and predict he has a golden future in movies. Brian Lowry of Hollywood *Variety* said the comedy was "slugglishly paced and too-seldom funny. Martin Lawrence's writer-director-producer-star turn in *A Thin Line Between Love and Hate* proves a tedious affair, alternately drawing its inspiration from *Boomerang* and *Fatal Attraction*."

On-set insiders said sparks were flying between Bobby and Ms. Whitfield, but he dismissed the reports as "the same kinda trash they're sayin' about my wife and Denzel." However, at the Los Angeles premiere of the movie in mid-April, Lynn Whitfield was on Bobby's arm, *not* Whitney!

That "same kinda trash" continued to follow Whitney and Denzel throughout the filming of *The Preacher's Wife*. As one studio executive put it, "It's just too juicy *not* to believe. Fans want to believe that the two most beautiful black stars of the nineties are falling in love."

Whitney's fans have always felt Bobby wasn't good enough for her, but Denzel Washington would be perfect. Not only is he handsome, but he's a clean-cut, straight-living, *nice* man. Longtime friends insist he's also a prude and say he has a long history of avoiding love scenes in movies. He balked at a graphic sex scene in Spike Lee's *Mo' Better Blues* and turned down the lead opposite Michelle Pfeiffer in the interracial romantic film *Love Field*. Starring with Julia Roberts in 1993's *The Pelican Brief*, he made sure their relationship was strictly platonic.

"Denzel's a shy guy," Kelly Lynch, his costar in *Virtuosity*, has said. "He nixed the idea of a love scene between us because he felt strongly that young white males wouldn't want to see him kissing me."

Producer Gary Lucchesi said, "It would never have worked for Denzel's character to pursue a romance with Kelly."

Director Carl Franklin agreed, claiming a love scene didn't fit, but "we would have done it if we could have made it work. Also, it was Denzel's choice. He didn't want the characters to have a romance."

In Denzel's newest release, *Devil in a Blue Dress*, with Jennifer Beals, again—no romance, even though the characters *do* have a torrid affair in Walter Mosley's novel on which the movie is based.

According to a friend of Denzel's (quoted anonymously on the Internet), "Hanging this around his neck isn't fair. This is a system that everybody knows about. A black man kissing a white woman in movies. You know who makes it the kiss of death? Studio executives. They think they're reflecting what the general public thinks it wants to see. White men made these rules."

Another friend thought differently: "It has nothing to do with interracial relationships. Denzel is a decent guy, he's kinda shy with women, and also, he's very much in love with his wife. It reminds me of when Pat Boone started making movies. He had it written into his contract he wouldn't have to do any love scenes."

Denzel has always proved just how much of a decent guy he is, and he's been rewarded for it. On January 14, 1996, he received the County of Los Angeles Board of Supervisors' prestigious Martin Luther King Jr. award, whose past honorees include Rosa Parks and San Francisco mayor Willie Brown. The organization also named the new pediatric wing at Los Angeles' Martin Luther King Jr. Hospital after Denzel, who has helped raise more than $4 million for South Central L.A. causes. Said a spokesman for the Board of Supervisors, "He could be out sipping mimosas, but instead he's here helping out."

Maybe all the current flap about the lack of black Oscar nominees (*People* magazine recently ran a cover story on the subject) had something to do with it, but suddenly the tragic life story of

Dorothy Dandridge is a hot property in Hollywood. Singer-actress Dandridge was the first black woman ever to be nominated for a Best Actress Oscar, for her role in 1954's *Carmen Jones,* and was universally admired for her beauty. Her personal life proved to be a riches-to-rags saga as she became an alcoholic and was forced into bankruptcy in the early sixties. Her penchant for white men landed her in the tabloids on a weekly basis, and she would often be booed onstage. She died in 1965 after mixing alcohol and sleeping pills.

Janet Jackson, who has long wanted to portray the singer-actress, paid tribute to Dandridge in her "Twenty Foreplay" video and has optioned the rights of a 1970 biography, *Everything and Nothing.*

But Whitney says *she* will play Dandridge and has bought the rights to an upcoming Amistad Press biography. She will also co-produce. Yet another acclaimed black actress wants the role, Halle Berry, and says she is "determined" to star in the movie. Debra Martin Chase, Whitney's production partner, said, "I sat next to Halle at a dinner recently and she said, 'If for any reason Whitney doesn't want to do it, tell her I'm *very* interested.' " But Whitney is hooked on the story and wants it for herself. "Dorothy had a lot to offer," she said. "She was a beautiful, beautiful woman."

Dandridge's story is the first acquisition for Whitney's film company, Houston Productions, which is based at Disney's Touchstone Pictures. "She was our [African American's] first goddess," Whitney says of Dandridge. "She deserves this tribute."

Commenting on the provocative *People*-magazine cover story "Hollywood Blackout," Whitney said she wasn't surprised that *Waiting to Exhale* was shut out of the nominations. "We were afraid, even when we were making the movie, that our work wouldn't be recognized at the Oscars. We talked about it on the set a lot. I mean, this is '96, and this has been going on for many, many years. What I'm going through today ain't nothing like what my brothers and sisters when through twenty, thirty years ago. So I'm kind of relieved of a lot of that pressure. We've kicked down doors before and we'll kick them down again."

As 1996 gets under way, Whitney is doing what she always does when under stress—working. Her calendar is full with concert dates, TV shows, movies, recordings, etc., while Bobby has only court dates lined up. At 3 A.M. Tuesday, April 23, 1996, in Atlanta, Georgia, he was stopped and arrested by police after they witnessed him speeding and swerving, according to Chuck Johnson, public information officer for the DeKalb County police. A woman was in the car with him (Geannie Ivey of Doraville, Georgia), who was not arrested, and Bobby told officers he had "picked her up in a bar."

According to the arresting officer's report, Bobby was asked to get out of the car and perform sobriety tests. "I noticed Brown was somewhat unsteady on his feet. I also saw him try to put his wallet away in his left front pants pocket. He missed the pocket and dropped the wallet to the ground." The officer said Brown swayed when he walked, and when asked to recite the alphabet, he named a few letters and then started over. On the third try, he recited the entire alphabet. The report went on to say that Brown had difficulty performing other sobriety tests as well, and he refused to take a breath test.

"I've already told you I've been drinking," Bobby told the officer. "I'm not going to tell on myself."

He was placed under arrest at that time and became "hostile and belligerent" when police read him his rights. He spent only a short time in jail and was released later in the day on $1,260 bail.

Bobby just can't seem to stay out of courthouses. Less than four months earlier, in December, he was sentenced to two years' probation on an assault and battery charge.

Whitney remains stoic, if somewhat tense, in defense of her husband. "You don't know what kind of a man he is unless you live with him and know him yourself. Bobby is the energy side of me and I'm the calm side of him, which works for us. I married the man I'm in love with. The person I can have fun with and be real with. This [marriage] isn't a game. It wasn't based on, 'Well, I need an R-and-B base and he needs some pop appeal.' People are so stupid."

As her marriage continues to stagger on and her staff continues to plead with the media to give her a break, Whitney doubles her workload. She's doing the sound track for *Preacher's Wife,* which will be all gospel numbers, and the movie is scheduled to finish about the end of May. Of all her many projects, this one is closest to her heart.

"When I come onto the set of this movie, its very spiritual," she told Beverly Hall Lawrence in a recent *TV Guide* interview. "Last week we had a choir here. We were doing our scenes together. I'm singing and the choir is singing, and all of a sudden it got out of hand where we couldn't control the spirit that took us over. And we just kept going and going. It wasn't a part of the movie, but it was a part of our feeling. Either you grow up with gospel or you don't."

I've kept in touch with a few members of the Royal Family, and they told me that Whitney is changing. She really is in love with Bobby and really does want the marriage to work. The affair didn't start out that way, as I've said before. At first, it was a ploy to make Robyn jealous, and also, I think, Whitney was sexually attracted to Bobby and his street-tough persona. He was dangerous and she found that a big turn-on. She had to be Little Miss Perfect all her life, especially in front of the media, so when she started stepping out openly with Bobby, it was as if she were saying, "See? I'm no white-bread princess. I can get down and dirty with the likes of Bobby Brown."

She is also going back to her roots, back to God and her love of gospel music. In an interview for *Harper's Bazaar* she told Sean Elder, "Gospel taught me to do a wide range of things: how to sing fast, how to sing slow, how to sing when the tempo changes in the middle of a song, how to sing four-part harmony without thinking about it. And how to sing without music, which is how you learn everything there is to know about music, in terms of your voice being the instrument, your feet being the drum, your hands—she begins clapping—being the tambourine."

I've heard Whitney sing numerous times, of course, but you really have to attend a concert to feel the soul in her voice. She told *Essence* magazine, "I love gospel. But does it make a record and does it have worldwide appeal? And what happens after that? Longevity—that's what it's all about. If you're going to have a long career, there's a certain way to do it, and I did it that way. I'm not ashamed of it. [Being referred to by critics as a white-bread crossover.] What's black? I've been trying to figure that out since I've been in the business. I don't know how to sing black and I don't know how to sing white, either. I just know how to sing. Music is not a color to me. It's an art." And she's not ashamed of her nonpop roots, either. In concert, she really cuts loose, and you can hear the gospel training and the soul tradition shining through.

A staff member told me, "She is both softer and tougher. I don't know how to explain it, but she's different. She don't take no kinda shit off nobody, that's for sure, but she's also sweeter since Bobbi Kris was born. She doesn't take chances like she used to. No more physical confrontations, no more fistfights with her brothers or Robyn. Somebody told me they thought she'd become a born-again Christian, but I don't know about that."

Whitney has always loved children, but since having one of her own, she seems to love them even more. VH1 honored her for her commitment to community causes in the form of the Whitney Houston Foundation for Children, which she founded in 1989. The foundation benefits, among others, Hale House, Rainbow House, and children's charities in South Africa.

She's hosting, for the second year in a row, Nickelodeon's Kids' Choice Awards. This is similar to the People's Choice Awards, except kids get to do the choosing, in categories from Favorite Song to Favorite TV Show and Favorite Performers. Last year, more than 26 million viewers telephoned, and this year voters can cast their choices through American Online or at their local McDonald's.

Whitney is up for the Hall of Fame Award this year (she's won in the past as well) and will preside over an hour-long show from Universal Studios Hollywood. Rosie O'Donnell will cohost, and presenters include the Olsen twins, Ashley and Mary Kate, Queen Latifah, and Nancy Kerrigan.

"I like to deal with kids, probably more than I like to deal with some adults," Whitney told *TV Guide.* "Kids don't pass judgment on you, because they don't come with all that baggage we adults do. I don't know about being a role model. I have lots of roles. But if I can just inspire them to look at what I've done and say, 'Well, if I get my education, if I'm inspired by the right people, then I can do what she did.' "

Whitney said she was interested in doing the Nickelodeon show because she can talk to the kids herself. "They read a lot of crap printed about me. It's just crap. And I don't want them to believe that is me. I can just wear jeans and sneakers and no one will tee off on my wardrobe. For once, I can just not worry about satisfying everyone's expectations."

She says this is the kind of wholesome programming she wants Bobbi Kris, whose current favorites are *Pocahontas* and *Sesame Street,* to watch. "When B.K. sees my videos, she claps and sings and dances along—but I don't necessarily want her to follow in my footsteps. If she's better at painting, then do that. If she's better at being a teacher or something else, do that. But if she wants to be in this business, I will be there to hold her hand.

"I just hope children will look at me and they will see things they can be inspired by. One day I won't be in this business and they will. I just hope that they learn." Asked where she saw herself in five years, she replied, "I don't really know if I see myself as a performing artist. I see myself developing other talents . . . contributing to helping the young accomplish their dreams."

In a special meeting arranged by *TV Guide,* Whitney agreed to be interviewed by three of her young fans, Ariel Osumenya, twelve, Jessica Wilson, thirteen, and Ria McCormick, also thirteen. The meeting took place at Sony Music Studios in New York City and would accompany the cover story in the May 4–10 issue of *TV Guide:*

ARIEL: I'm a singer and want to become a professional. What advice do you have for me?

WHITNEY: Get ready for the work, 'cause it takes a lot of work. And it's not always about the fame and fortune, it's about loving what you do. If you love what you do, and you inspire others to do great things, that's really worth it for me. Sitting here with you is worth it to me. And get ready to not be paid as much as you think you should be paid.

RIA: How does fame affect your life?

WHITNEY: It takes a lot of your time and your privacy away. Things that you usually might do, like going to the movies or to a restaurant cannot be done. People would come up and ask for your autograph. And I always have to go out with a bodyguard.

JESSICA: Which people inspired you to sing and perform? Did you have any role models?

WHITNEY: My mother was a key person. I had her, as someone who was a mother but also someone in the business who could guide me. Young people need a lot of guidance, with all the money and everything. They don't know enough. I always talk about the business and the importance of understanding the legalities of the business. She didn't want me to be in show business, but I'm what you call a show-business kid.

For the cover shot for *TV Guide,* Whitney is dressed in a snappy black leather pants suit with high-heeled black boots, but for the meeting with the three girls she is casual in blue jeans, white blouse, and black suede loafers. Interviewer Beverly Hall Lawrence admits it was an unexpected image to see the diva of pop so open and friendly with the girls, at times giggling like a teenager herself as they talked.

Suddenly, one of the awestruck girls blurted out, "I've loved you since I was two!" and Whitney was momentarily stunned. "I hear her saying 'since I was two,' and they're twelve or thirteen, and I say, 'Dag, I've been out there *that long*? I've been out here about thirteen years. I'm trying to maintain just being myself. I don't try to be someone I'm not."

For these three starstruck girls, two of whom attend a public performing-arts school, Whitney is the epitome of everything they aspire to. She has both an extraordinary singing career (over 80 million records sold worldwide) and a hot, up-and-coming career as movie star, commanding $10 million per picture.

18

A New Whitney Houston

JUST WHEN IT SEEMED WHITNEY WAS TURNING HER LIFE AROUND and finally getting it together, a story appeared in the *Globe* about her half brother, Gary Garland. He had been arrested with five rocks of crack cocaine in his possession. He violently resisted, trying to pull free of the police officers and run as they were handcuffing him. He was released a couple of days later on $11,000 bail.

I called a friend when I read about the arrest and wondered if Gary was buying the crack for Whitney to lace her joints with. He said, "No way! She's finally growing up and getting some sense." All the troubles Bobby had had with the law had made a profound impression on her. She didn't want drugs and violence in her life, especially now that she has a child. She wants more children and a happy marriage and a normal, sane existence.

I spoke to a few other people who were close to Whitney and they told me the same thing. The arrogant, cold, belligerent diva who could wither a fan with a sneer was growing a heart. She was kinder to her staff, considerate of others, and genuinely concerned with doing good works. She now felt with her enormous popularity she should give some thing back to her fans who had been so loyal to her, and she proved it to me in a big way.

I was watching the *Leeza* show on television April 19. Host Leeza Gibbons was devoting the entire show to the one-year anniversary of the Oklahoma City bombing and had several of the survivors onstage to tell about their experiences. Dana L. Cooper was there and told about being trapped under all the debris that had fallen on her from a collapsed upper floor. One of her legs had been pinned beneath tons of twisted metal, and rescuers could not free her. A doctor, hearing of her plight, rushed to the scene and, lying on his stomach amid the dirt and rubble, amputated her leg with his pocketknife.

Ms. Cooper was soft-spoken and shy when Leeza questioned her about her ordeal. She showed little emotion until Leeza asked her who her favorite singer was, then she became animated and smiled broadly, saying, "Whitney Houston."

"Well, guess what?" Leeza said. "She's on the phone and wants to talk to you."

The audience went wild, cheering, clapping, stomping so loudly it was difficult to hear Whitney's first few words. She spoke directly to Dana Cooper, telling her how brave she was and how strong to withstand something so tragic. Whitney praised her for her courage and said she knew God had been with her and that God was her protector and would always bless and keep her safe. Whitney said she couldn't imagine the strength it must have taken to undergo surgery in such a primitive fashion without drugs to kill the pain. She said God must have something very special in mind for Dana, and several times she murmured softly, "Bless you, girl, bless you and may God keep you safe." She said if Dana ever needed "anything, anything at all, just call me. If I can do *anything* for you, you let me know, you hear? I'll be there for you."

The studio audience roared its approval as Leeza promised to get Whitney's new CD to Dana, then the screen was filled with a still photograph of Whitney, looking like an angel. Lit from behind, her lovely face was surrounded by a soft, golden aura, and her eyes were soft and kind, and I was struck dumb. Gone was the hard-eyed, glittering beauty I had come to recognize in publicity stills. This was a grown woman with tenderness and compassion in her face, and I can't tell you how great that made me feel. I had always hoped that Whitney would realize how blessed she was and use her good fortune to help others. Now there she was on national TV extending a helping hand to a middle-class, ordinary black woman whose life had been changed forever by a brutally violent act of cruelty. But just hearing Whitney's voice had cheered her so much and put a smile on her face that hadn't been there before. It was a touching moment for me.

Ever since my split from the Royal Family I had been trying to get my life back on an even keel. I founded an organization called the Power Club and am currently working with Danny Davis, city commissioner of Chicago, to promote positive messages. I recognized the negative effects on both the community and local businesses when children lack positive activities. The Power Club initiated the Sharing the World With Our Kids program. We provide productive outlets for children to become involved in their community and to participate in group activities on out-of-school holidays and during the summer months. The program is open to anyone, regardless of age, color, sex religion, or national origin.

My purpose in founding this program was to offer underprivileged inner-city kids the opportunity to experience the diversity and richness of Chicago's culture, architecture, cuisine, and, shopping. In addition, it provides a much-needed respite from the everyday violence on our streets and in our schools.

The program targets kids between the ages of five and fifteen, who are chosen from elementary and high school throughout the city. They are chosen on the basis of their needs and their ability to benefit from the cultural awareness trips. Most of these youngsters have never been exposed to anything other than violence and poverty, so these cultural trips teach them how to work within a group of peers without the competition for "turf" and for acceptance that confronts them daily in their gang-ridden environment. We're all committed to building a comprehensive, coordinated system of support for positive youth development.

I felt so much better about myself when I started replacing the anger and sense of betrayal I had held against Whitney and the whole Houston family for their shabby treatment of me. When I saw Whitney on TV and saw the change in her, it somehow eased my own pain. I could understand her better and I could finally forgive her.

In March 1996, I participated in the Million Man March in Washington, D.C., and I'm also working on opening another program for the youth of Chicago called the Social Service Center. My first love is still music and I continue to sing whenever and wherever I get a chance. For the past two years I've been producing a newsletter called *What's Hot and What's Not,* which has really caught on in Chicago. At a glance, people can see what's happening in their city, the top radio station and DJ, the boss record, the best movie or TV show, the hottest place to go for dinner or entertainment.

It also has a weekly horoscope and an advice column written by the "Love Doctor." The success has been phenomenal, and my office was flooded with calls after just the first issue. I'm thinking of having it distributed in New York, Atlanta, Los Angeles, and Detroit as well. At first, I thought of it as a vehicle for advertisements and my first printing was fifty thousand, but now its become a sort of mini-entertainment-a-glance success story. I run the names of my sponsors along both sides of the newsletter, and the companies tell me they've increased their business twofold.

I wasn't surprised when Regina Brown called and wanted me to run her advertisement for her new business, Brown & Associates: Special Event Consultants. I did, for several months, and never got paid a dime. She was still the same old Regina. And she was still up to her old tricks of selling personal information to the tabloids.

Not long ago I was contacted by an attorney for the *New York Post* wanting me to testify on their behalf against Regina, Whitney, and Flo Anthony regarding a story that Regina had sold. I turned them down. I don't want anything to do with Regina. She called my mother and told her she was still in love with me and her marriage was "in name only" and she wanted me back in her life. She was crying and begging my mother to talk to me and to make me understand how much she loved me and needed me. It didn't work. Thank God, my wife forgave me and our marriage is now stronger than ever. We have a new baby son and life is good again.

I still keep in touch with some of the people I met while traveling with Whitney, and I will never give up my dream of some day recording an album of my songs, but this time I'll do it on my own. I won't wait for someone else to make it happen for me. I still speak with Michael pretty often, and we get together when he's in Chicago. I've also remained good friends with L. L. Cool J, and he always calls when he's in town, so I guess a couple of good things came out of my nightmare with the Royal Family.

When I saw that Lynn Whitfield was in the movie *A Thin Line Between Love and Hate*, I thought, *Uh-oh*. Bobby and Lynn used to be very tight, even though he was dating Whitney at the time. I was first aware of it at the Black Achievement Awards in 1991. I could see some flirting going on, and I could see that Whitney was getting a little hot under the collar. Finally, Whitney confronted Lynn. I didn't hear all of the conversation, but I did hear Whitney call Lynn a "bitch" and tell her to stay away from my man or "I'll kick your ass!" Now the press was reporting that sparks were flying on the set and that it was Bobby who had suggested hiring Lynn for the movie. I hoped Whitney's new "kinder, gentler" personality would win out over the old, hostile one when she saw the pictures of Bobby escorting Lynn to the premiere of the movie.

"I don't think she even gave it a second thought," a friend told me. "She's so used to Bobby making a fool of himself in public, she just looks the other way."

Everyone I spoke with told me pretty much the same thing; Whitney had grown and changed and she wants to put all the trash behind her and get on with her life. And what a life it's been! She became a huge recording star while still a teenager, then a mega-super movie star after her film debut in *The Bodyguard*. Unfortunately, that brought all manner of unwanted publicity and unflattering speculation. She's been called everything from a could, heartless calculating hit-making machine to a mindless, robotlike creation of Svengali Clive Davis. It seems critics are unaware of her terrific voice, a megawatt, three-octave wonder that probably had *something* to do with her success!

While researching this book, I discovered Whitney had appeared on two television sitcoms, *Gimme a Break* (staring Nell Carter) and *Silver Spoons* (with Joel Higgins and a very young Ricky Schroder), both of which were big hits in the 1980s. She made her singing debut on *The Merv Griffin Show* before cutting a single record and is now coming full circle by hosting the Kids' Choice Awards on Nickelodeon.

She also seems to have changed her attitude toward reporters as well. In the beginning of her career she was flattered by the attention and spoke openly in interviews, telling the truth about her feelings until she discovered that reporters are notorious for misquoting stars; then she became wary and suspicious. "Hostile and rude" was the way most reporters saw it. Almost everyone who interviewed her had prejudged her as nothing more than the new "flavor of the month," a beautiful face but no personality to speak of, nothing that would distinguish her from any other pretty young singer out there. But they came away very much surprised at what a strong, opinionated, *smart* woman she really is.

"Family is very important to Whitney," Deborah Schindler, producer of *Waiting to Exhale*, has said. "She surrounds herself with people who are protective of her, a comfort zone."

"My family is my guidance," Whitney is fond of saying. She likes the word *guidance* and has used it a number of times in her interviews, especially when referring to the influential men in her life. "He is my guidance," she has said of Kevin Costner, Clive Davis, Babyface, and Forest Whitaker. She elaborates on Whitaker, saying the success of *Exhale* was due not only to his expert direction, but his "guidance."

"He has such a peaceful demeanor—and only a man with a peaceful demeanor could have dealt with four feisty African-American women! And such a quiet temperament, very even all the time. When he got upset, he took long walks and then would come back. And I thought, this is a very special guy."

Whitney herself is striving for that same kind of quiet temperament and has dedicated her video "Miracle" to all the miracles, big and small, that change peoples lives or change the world in some way. She has said she wants the Whitney Houston Foundation to celebrate hope, to give children a belief in miracles. "I want them to believe their smallest personal triumphs are important so they will strive for bigger triumphs in life and never give up."

She has always lived by that rule and has never given up on anything she wants either personally or professionally. "I do know you have to put God first," she has said. "And if you put Him first, and you come to Him, anything can be worked out. He's a problem solver. He's proved it to me every time."

I hope He proves it to her again with her shaky marriage to Bobby, but I really doubt it. Not for anything Whitney has done or failed to do, but because Bobby doesn't seem to want it as much as she does. Maybe if his career takes off and he starts getting some recognition and success of his own, it will change things. Whitney has said she plans on taking a "nice, long, quiet vacation" when *Preacher's Wife* wraps at the end of May, and then "we'll work our problems out. Not *we* and the world, just the two of us."

I was talking to a friend about one of Whitney's old boyfriends, restaurateur Brad Johnson, who is now in a heavy romance with Sharon Stone, and I remembered rumor had it that Brad had broken Whitney's heart back then. I wondered what she thought of his falling for a femme-fatale heartbreaker like Ms. Stone, and my friend said, "She wishes both every happiness."

In *People* magazine's annual "50 Most Beautiful People in the World" issue, Whitney wasn't listed while her *Exhale* costar Lela Rochon was. So was her *Preacher's Wife* costar Denzel Washington. I asked my source how she felt about that, and he said, "She don't give a damn about stuff like that. She never did bank on her looks. I'm telling you, Kevin, she's changed. All she thinks about now is Bobbi Kris and how she can make her life happier. She has such wonderful plans and dreams for that little girl, and one of them is to give her a brother or sister in the near future. Hopefully, with Bobby Brown."

I was so glad to hear all the positive reports I was getting about Whitney. I had grown fond of her during my time with the Royal Family and I wished her only the best. It's true that I felt betrayed by her when she went back on her word to help me get a record deal, but in retrospect, I guess it was wrong to expect someone else to just hand me my dream. Everybody has to pay his own dues.

The time I spent with Whitney was beneficial in many ways, and I learned a lot about life on the road with a superstar. While traveling with her and putting up with the constant fights, both physical and verbal, between her and Robyn and the rest of the Royal Family, I had secretly called it the Tour From Hell and had yearned for my quiet life back in Chicago. But now that I have that quiet life, I miss the excitement. I miss the limousines and fancy restaurants and high living and rubbing elbows with celebrities. I miss the high I always got when I watched Whitney rehearsing for a concert, and I miss the anticipation that I always felt when she promised me a recording contract and told me she knew I would be a star someday.

Maybe I will be. I don't know. But I feel I'm a better person for having gone through all I did with Whitney. I know I learned a lot about myself that maybe I wouldn't have had to face had it not been for my close encounter with the likes of John Houston. I don't even hate *him* anymore. I feel pity for him because he's the last of a dying breed of bullies and control freaks who think they can go through life scaring people into doing their dirty work for them. Whitney had a lot of that controlling trait in her makeup, too, but thank God she's breaking the cycle. Now that she's a mother herself, perhaps she's kinder to her mother. I hope she is showing Cissy more respect these days and has forgiven her for the mistakes she made when Whitney was a child.

Cissy was just as headstrong and demanding as John was, but I never disliked her. I was amused by her. She was so full of strutting self-importance, so egocentric, just so taken by *herself,* that I was always hiding a grin behind my hand. But now I don't think it was so funny. It was really pathetic because she's had to face the death of a lifelong dream, stardom, and see it bestowed upon her daughter a thousandfold.

Not long ago Michael told me he was just as surprised and happy as I was hearing about all the changes in his sister. She would never give him a break in the music business, but she's always taken care of him financially and for that he is grateful. He was getting a weekly paycheck of $250, certainly not a great amount but enough to get along. I recently tried to call him and was told he was in rehab—again. Both he and Gary have been in and out of rehabilitation centers for drug abuse several times, and every time I pray that this time it works. Michael is a good, decent guy in so many ways, and I'd like to see him get his act together once and for all. He has an excellent voice, and I think if he let go of Whitney's coattails, he'd make it as a singer in his own right.

Lately, every time I read an entertainment magazine, some reviewer is praising the movie *The Preacher's Wife* and already predicting it will be another megahit for Whitney when it is released during the Christmas season in 1996. No one is surprised by Denzel's sterling performance because he has proved himself a brilliant actor in every movie he has appeared in, but they are saying that Whitney is "surprisingly effective" and "shows great promise as a leading lady" and that her "ethereal beauty lights up the theater" . . . when she is on-screen, "you can't take your eyes off her."

And several times reporters have summed up their glowing comments by adding, "Now if only she can get her personal life in order, there will be no stopping this talented young woman."

In a recent man-on-the-street interview hosted by E! Entertainment television, people were asked how they felt about various stars, and several Whitney Houston fans said, "Whitney's got it goin' on—now if she'd just get rid of that loser husband of hers . . ."

Public opinion of Bobby has not changed for the better, even though he was praised for his acting in *A Thin Line Between Love and Hate*. If anything, it has gotten worse as he continues to get into scrapes with the law. Most articles written about him begin, "Trouble magnet Bobby Brown had another run-in with police . . ." Friends say the short stay at the Betty Ford Clinic did not take and he's back to his old habits of drinking and drugging.

"Personally, I think it's his youth combined with his rough childhood of growing up in the gangs," one friend told me. "Guys in the 'hood tend to think sobriety is sissy, and they're used to doing any fucking thing they want to do. Period. I think Bobby's just rebelling against being told that he *has* to stop drinking. He's always been a hothead and he's still a kid in many ways, even though he's now—what?—about twenty-six, twenty-seven? He didn't have any time to be a kid when he *was* a kid, so I think he's just tryin' to cram a whole lot of fun into his life while he's got the chance."

Being married to the biggest superstar in the business gives him ample opportunity to have fun. He lives in a mansion, drives a Bentley or Rolls-Royce or any other luxury car of his choice. Somebody told me Whitney has a new black Rolls, a Porsche, a lavender limousine, a gold Bentley, and an assortment of other top-of-the-line automobiles, which are all at Bobby's disposal whenever he wants to drive them.

I can understand how that kind of life turns his head, and I can see where he finds it difficult to stay sober around the people he hangs out with. Also, when you're a celebrity, fans give you drugs—all the time. I've seen women and guys rush up to singers and movie stars and shove Baggies of pot and envelopes of cocaine into their hands, hoping the celebrity will remember them and think better of them. It's like a conspiracy of sorts, a camaraderie, like, "Wow! So and so is smokin' *my* pot or snortin' *my* coke."

Stars get free drinks sent to them by management and fans alike when they go out to a restaurant, and reporters send them bottles of expensive booze in the hopes they will agree to an interview. Business associates, record companies, and movie studios send $150 bottles of brandy or $200 bottles of champagne either to thank their stars or to woo new ones. It's hard to say no to all that attention, and apparently Bobby doesn't want to, but I'm so proud to hear that Whitney now wants a drug-free life for herself. She could just as easily have gone the way of other stars whose meteoric rise to fame threw them into a tailspin of self-destruction, but she caught herself in time. Like the fan said on TV: "Whitney's got it goin' on."

At age thirty-two, after only thirteen shorts years in the business, Whitney Houston is still on top of the heap. Her reviews now call her global, international, out of this galaxy, the most famous black superstar in history—and the only thing I have left to say is, "Way to go, Nippy!"

Index